lonely planet

Pocket
COPENHAGEN

TOP SIGHTS • LOCAL LIFE • MADE EASY

D0017989

Cristian Bonetto

In This Book

QuickStart Guide

Your keys to understanding the city – we help you decide what to do and how to do it

Need to Know
Tips for a smooth trip

Neighbourhoods
What's where

Explore Copenhagen

The best things to see and do, neighbourhood by neighbourhood

Top Sights
Make the most of your visit

Local Life
The insider's city

The Best of Copenhagen

The city's highlights in handy lists to help you plan

Best Walks
See the city on foot

Copenhagen's Best...
The best experiences

Survival Guide

Tips and tricks for a seamless, hassle-free city experience

Getting Around
Travel like a local

Essential Information
Including useful websites

Our selection of the city's best places to eat, drink and experience:

◎ **Sights**

✖ **Eating**

🚇 **Drinking**

⭐ **Entertainment**

🔒 **Shopping**

These symbols give you the vital information for each listing:

☏ Telephone Numbers	👪	Family-Friendly
⊙ Opening Hours	🐾	Pet-Friendly
P Parking	🚌	Bus
Ⓝ Nonsmoking	🚢	Ferry
@ Internet Access	M	Metro
🛜 Wi-Fi Access	S	Subway
🥗 Vegetarian Selection	⊖	London Tube
🅜 English-Language Menu	🚋	Tram
	🚆	Train

Find each listing quickly on maps for each neighbourhood:

Bar Hemingway

16 🚇 Map p233, B2

Legend has it that Hemi
self, wielding a machine
rate this timber-pan
ered bar during
showpiece is a
en by Papa ar
town. Dress
s.com; Hôtel Rit
⊙6.30pm-2a

Lonely Planet's Copenhagen

Lonely Planet Pocket Guides are designed to get you straight to the heart of the city.

Inside you'll find all the must-see sights, plus tips to make your visit to each one really memorable. We've split the city into easy-to-navigate neighbourhoods and provided clear maps so you'll find your way around with ease. Our expert authors have searched out the best of the city: walks, food, nightlife and shopping, to name a few. Because you want to explore, our 'Local Life' pages will take you to some of the most exciting areas to experience the real Copenhagen.

And of course you'll find all the practical tips you need for a smooth trip: itineraries for short visits, how to get around, and how much to tip the guy who serves you a drink at the end of a long day's exploration.

It's your guarantee of a really great experience.

Our Promise

You can trust our travel infor-mation because Lonely Planet authors visit the places we write about, each and every edition. We never accept freebies for positive coverage, so you can rely on us to tell it like it is.

QuickStart Guide **7**

Copenhagen Top Sights......**8**

Copenhagen Local Life......**12**

Copenhagen Day Planner...**14**

Need to Know......**16**

Copenhagen Neighbourhoods......**18**

Explore Copenhagen **21**

22 Tivoli Area

34 Slotsholmen

44 Strøget & Around

58 Nyhavn & The Royal Quarter

70 Christianshavn

82 Nørreport

96 Nørrebro

108 Vesterbo

Worth a Trip:

Østerbro......**106**

Frederiksberg......**120**

Louisiana Museum of Modern Art......**122**

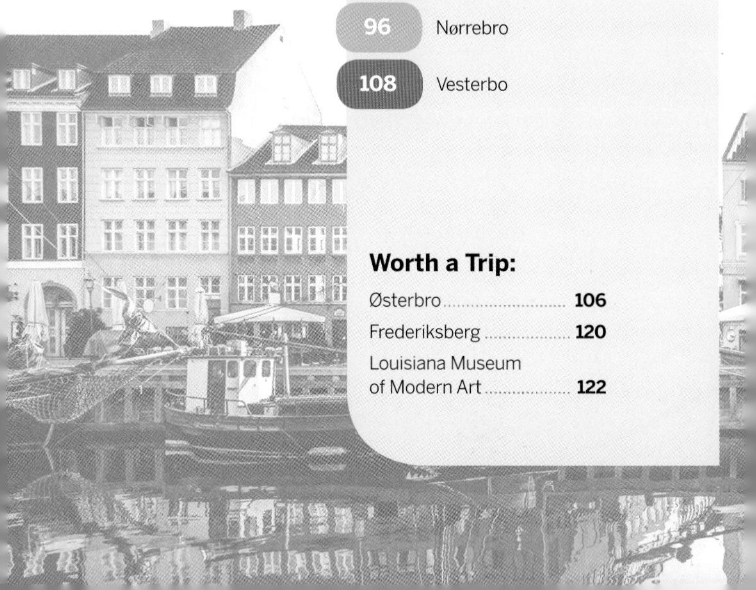

The Best of Copenhagen 125

Copenhagen's Best Walks

Slotsholmen Saunter 126

Nørrebro Soul 128

Copenhagen's Best ...

Museums & Galleries 130

Shopping 132

Eating 134

Drinking 136

Entertainment 137

Hygge 138

For Free 139

Tours 140

For Kids 141

Architecture 142

Design 143

Festivals & Events 144

Survival Guide 145

Before you go 146

Arriving in Copenhagen ... 147

Getting Around 148

Essential Information 149

Language 152

QuickStart Guide

Copenhagen Top Sights 8

Copenhagen Local Life 12

Copenhagen Day Planner 14

Need to Know.. 16

Copenhagen Neighbourhoods.............................. 18

Welcome to Copenhagen

Compact Copenhagen is the epitome of Scandi cool. Modernist lamps light New Nordic tables, bridges buzz with cycling commuters and eye-candy locals dive into pristine waterways. Despite the cobbled streets, whimsical spires and palaces, this is a city at the very cutting edge, bursting with boundary-pushing food, design and fashion. Go on, take a bite of the (sustainable) good life.

Christianshavn (p70)

©EUGENE ANBALL/500PX ©

Copenhagen
Top Sights

Tivoli Gardens (p24)

Amusement rides, music and fireworks.

Nationalmuseet (p28)

A crash course in Danish history.

Christiansborg Slot (p36)

Tapestries, ruins and commanding views.

Designmuseum Danmark

(p60) Vintage and modern Danish design.

Christiania (p72)

A free-spirited commune.

Rosenborg Slot (p84)
Christian IV's Renaissance castle.

Statens Museum for Kunst (p88) Denmark's top-tier art museum.

Louisiana Museum of Modern Art (p122) Modern art by the Baltic.

○ Copenhagen
Local Life

Local experiences and hidden gems
to help you uncover the real city

Beyond Copenhagen's celebrated museums, landmarks and waterfront is the city the locals live and love – a multifaceted place of Nordic market produce, whimsical street art, grit-hip bars and tranquil, romantic gardens.

Torvehallerne KBH (p90)
☑ Gourmet bites ☑ Artisan produce

KIEV.VICTOR/SHUTTERSTOCK ©

Østerbro (p106)
☑ Heritage architecture ☑ Cosy cafes and eateries

Frederiksberg (p120)

☑ Romantic parks ☑ Subterranean art

Other great places to experience the city like a local:

Dansk Arkitektur Center (p142)

Café Halvvejen (p51)

Bastard Café (p52)

Cinemateket (p55)

Forloren Espresso (p67)

Islands Brygge Havnebadet (p139)

Superkilen (p128)

Manfreds og Vin (p102)

Dyrehaven (p118)

Cykelslangen (p119)

Continental Værnedamsvej (p110)

☑ Street life ☑ Food and drink

Copenhagen
Day Planner

Day One

Pique your appetite at **Torve-hallerne KBH** (p90), Copenhagen's celebrated food market. Warm up with porridge at Grød, browse Danish edibles at Bornholmer Butikken and Omegn, and slurp superlative brew at Coffee Collective. Walk over to **Kongens Have** (p87), a former royal backyard turned city park. Snoop around the Hogwarts-worthy rooms of its 17th-century castle, **Rosenborg Slot** (p84), home to the Danish crown jewels.

Continue east to salty **Nyhavn** (p64). Capture the perfect snap of the colourful canal, then hop on a canal-and-harbour tour of the city. Alternatively, walk north along the harbourfront to royal pad **Amalienborg Slot** (p64), the glorious church **Marmorkirken** (p64) and, further north, fortress **Kastellet** (p65). If you must, the **Little Mermaid** (p66) awaits a short walk away from Kastellet. Once done, catch a Harbour Bus south to **Det Kongelige Bibliotek** (p41).

Spend the evening at **Tivoli Gardens** (p24). If it's Friday night between mid-April and late September, you'll be just in time for Tivoli's popular Fredagsrock at Plænen, music concerts often featuring prolific local or international acts.

Day Two

Start on a high by climbing **Rundetårn** (p48), a 17th-century tower with views fit for its founder, Christian IV. The streets directly to the east – among them Pilestræde and Gammel Mønt – are dotted with Nordic fashion boutiques, such as **Wood Wood** (p57) and **Han Kjøbenhavn** (p57), as well as Scandi design stores like **Hay House** (p55). Alternatively, explore the streets southwest of Rundetårn, which together form the historic **Latin Quarter** (p48). It's here that you'll find **Vor Frue Kirke** (p48), home to sculptures by the great Bertel Thorvaldsen.

You could easily spend the afternoon exploring Danish history at the **Nationalmuseet** (p28). If impressionist brushstrokes appeal more, opt for **Ny Carlsberg Glyptotek** (p31), one of the city's finest art museums and home to the biggest booty of Rodin sculptures outside of France.

Continue the night with elegant wine, conversation and classic Danish design at **Ved Stranden 10** (p51), innovative cocktails at **Ruby** (p52) or maybe some evening sax at **Jazzhouse** (p53) or **Jazzhus Montmartre** (p53).

Short on time?
We've arranged Copenhagen's must-sees into these day-by-day itineraries to make sure you see the very best of the city in the time you have available.

Day Three

☀ Spend the morning exploring Christianshavn. If it's open, pop into **Christians Kirke** (p78) to eye-up its theatre-like interior. Architectural curiosity also underscores **Vor Frelsers Kirke** (p77), topped by a spiral wooden tower. Both are within walking distance of **Christiania** (p72). Get off its infamous main drag – dubbed Pusher St – and take in the commune's organic architecture.

☀ After lunch, cross Knippelsbro (Knippels Bridge) to reach Slotsholmen. The island's protagonist is **Christiansborg Slot** (p36), whose breathtaking **De Kongelige Repræsentationslokaler** (p36) are worth a visit. Directly below are the **Ruinerne under Christiansborg** (p37), which include traces of the city's original 12th-century castle. For Danish sculpture and classical antiquities, drop into **Thorvaldsens Museum** (p41).

☾ Kick back in Kødbyen, the city's on-trend 'Meatpacking District'. While the district is home to numerous bars – including **Mesteren & Lærlingen** (p118) – wrap things up at craft-beer standouts **Mikkeller Bar** (p118) and **Fermentoren** (p118), or cocktail hideout **Lidkoeb** (p117).

Day Four

☀ Delve into masterpieces both old and cutting edge at **Statens Museum for Kunst** (p88). This is Denmark's national gallery, home to artworks by Danish giants like Vilhelm Hammershøi, Asger Jorn and Per Kirkeby, as well as one of the world's finest collections of works by Matisse. If you need to clear your head, the canvas-worthy **Botanisk Have** (p93) is just across the road.

☀ Spend the afternoon exploring Copenhagen's densest, coolest, most multicultural neighbourhood, Nørrebro. Amble streets like Jægersborggade, Elmegade and Guldbergsgade for boutiques and studios peddling anything from local ceramics and fashion to retro Danish lamps. When it's time to pause, people-watch in out-of-the-box urban park **Superkilen** (p128) or take a nap in dreamy **Assistens Kirkegård** (p99).

☾ Keep the night rolling at Nørrebro's plethora of idiosyncratic drinking holes, among them craft-beer hotspots **Brus** (p102) and **Mikkeller & Friends** (p102) or the perennially soulful **Kind of Blue** (p104). For live music and late-week clubbing sessions, hit **Rust** (p103).

Need to Know

**For more information,
see Survival Guide (p145)**

Currency
Danish krone (kr)

Language
Danish; English widely spoken

Money
ATMs widely available.
Credit cards accepted in most hotels,
restaurants and shops. Some businesses
accept cards, not cash.

Mobile Phones
Mobile coverage is widespread. Non-EU
residents should bring a GSM-compatible
phone; local SIM cards are available.

Time
Central European Time
(GMT/UTC plus one hour)

Tipping
Rare and not expected at hotels. Consider
tipping 10% of the bill for exceptional service
at restaurants and consider rounding up the
fare in taxis.

① Before You Go

Your Daily Budget

Budget: Less than 800kr
▶ Dorm bed: 150–300kr
▶ Double room in budget hotel: 500–700kr
▶ Cheap meal: under 125kr

Midrange: 800–1500kr
▶ Double room in midrange hotel: 700–1500kr
▶ Museum admission: 50–150kr
▶ Three-course menu 300-400kr

Top end: More than 1500kr
▶ Double room in top-end hotel: 1500kr and up
▶ Degustation menu at Kadeau: 1800kr

Useful Websites

Visit Copenhagen (www.visitcopenhagen.com) Covers everything from accommodation and sightseeing to dining, shopping and events.

Rejseplanen (www.rejseplanen.dk) Useful journey planner.

Lonely Planet (www.lonelyplanet.com/copenhagen) Destination information, hotel bookings, traveller forum and more.

Advance Planning

Two months before Book your hotel and a table at restaurant Kadeau (p78).

One to two weeks before Secure a table at hotspot restaurants like Restaurant Mes (p32), Bror (p32) and Höst (p94).

Few days before Scan www.visitcopenhagen.com and www.aok.dk for upcoming events.

② Arriving in Copenhagen

Most people arrive by air, landing at Copenhagen Airport, Scandinavia's busiest international airport. A smaller number of international visitors arrive in Copenhagen by train to Central Station, by long-distance bus or by ferry.

✈ From Copenhagen Airport

Trains run to the city centre around every 10 to 20 minutes, with fewer services overnight. Metro trains also run to the city centre every four to 20 minutes, 24 hours a day. Taxis to the city centre cost around 250kr to 300kr.

🚊 From Central Station

All regional and international trains arrive at and depart from Central Station (København H), located in the heart of the city. Trains run to the airport every 10 to 20 minutes, with less frequent services overnight. Most long-distance buses terminate on Ingerslevsgade, at the southern end of Central Station.

⚓ From Søndre Frihavn

Cruise ferries to and from Norway dock at Søndre Frihavn, located 2km north of Kongens Nytorv. Bus 26 connects the port to the city centre and Vesterbro.

③ Getting Around

Copenhagen has an extensive public transit system consisting of a metro, train, bus and ferry network.

🚲 Bike

Most streets have cycle lanes and, more importantly, motorists tend to respect them. Bikes can be carried free on S-trains, but are forbidden at Nørreport station during weekday peak times. Bikes are also banned on the metro during weekday peak times.

🚌 Bus

Extensive coverage. Primary routes have an 'A' after their route number and run 24 hours a day, every three to seven minutes in peak times and every 10 minutes at other times. Night buses (marked with an 'N' after their route number) run between 1am and 5am.

Metro

Two lines, M1 and M2. Services run around the clock: every two to four minutes in peak times, three to six minutes during the day and on weekends, and seven to 20 minutes at night. Both lines connect Nørreport with Kongens Nytorv and Christianshavn. Line M2 runs to the airport. A city-circle line is due for completion in 2019.

🚊 Train

Known locally as S-tog, Copenhagen's suburban train network runs seven lines through Central Station (København H). Services run every four to 20 minutes from approximately 5am to 12.30am. All-night services run hourly on Friday and Saturday (half-hourly on line F).

⚓ Ferry

The city's commuter ferries are known as Harbour Buses. There are 10 stops along the harbourfront.

Copenhagen
Neighbourhoods

Worth a Trip
◉ Top Sights
Louisiana

Nørrebro (p96)
Copenhagen at its graffiti-scrawled best, jam-packed with indie cafes and rocking retro treasures and buried national legends.

Tivoli Area (p22)
Copenhagen's bustling 'welcome mate', home to the cultural blockbuster Nationalmuseet and ageless charmer Tivoli Gardens.

◉ Top Sights
Tivoli Gardens

Nationalmuseet

Vesterbro (p108)
The pinnacle of Copenhagen cool, where post-industrial bars, eateries and galleries mix it with vintage thrift shops and the odd porn peddler.

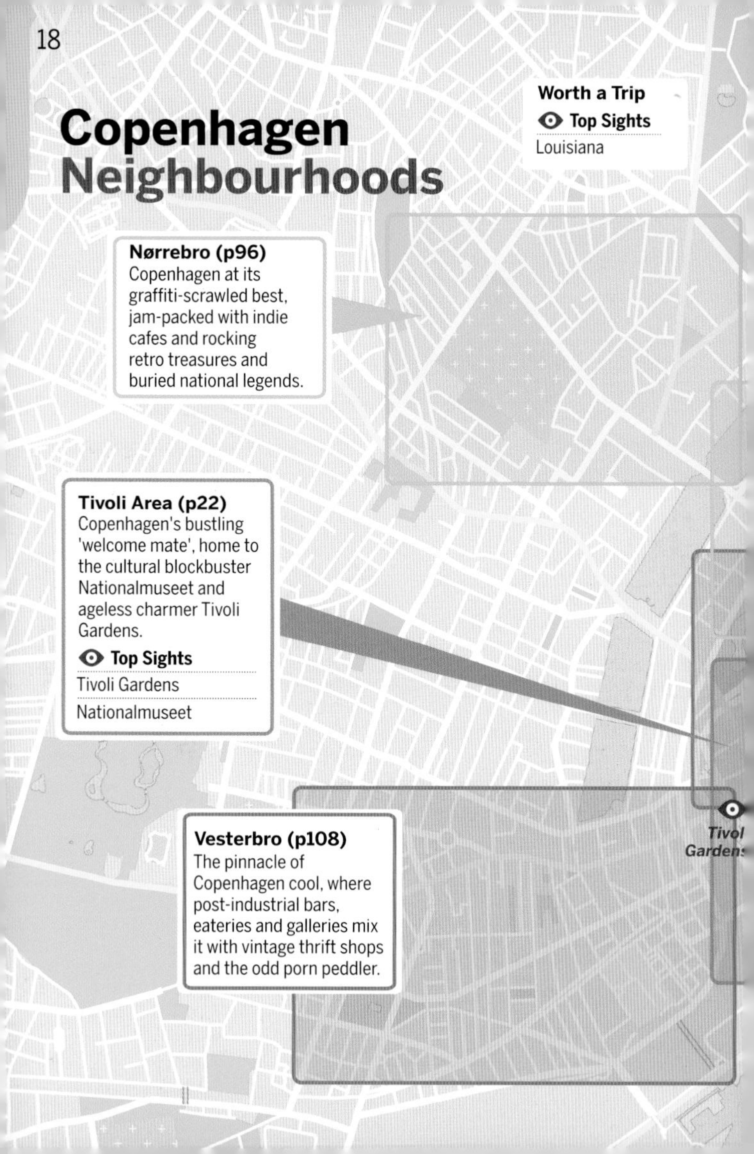

◉
Tivoli Gardens

Nørreport (p82)

An appetite-piquing, soul-stirring feast of market produce, artistic masterpieces, royal turrets and jewels, and dashing parklands.

◉ Top Sights

Rosenborg Slot

Statens Museum for Kunst

Strøget & Around (p44)

Nordic fashion flagships, buzzing cafes and bars, and twisting cobbled streets draw the crowds in Copenhagen's historic heart.

Nyhavn & the Royal Quarter (p58)

Masts and maritime buildings, a rococo royal palace and the world's most famous mermaid – welcome to the city of postcard images.

◉ Top Sights

Designmuseum Danmark

Christianshavn (p70)

Scandinavia's answer to Amsterdam, pimped with cosy canals, boats and cafes, and the pot-scented streets of alt-living commune Christiania.

◉ Top Sights

Christiania

Statens Museum for Kunst ◉

Designmuseum Danmark ◉

◉
Rosenborg Slot

◉
Christiansborg Slot

◉
Nationalmuseet

Christiania ◉

Slotsholmen (p34)

Parliamentary palace, medieval ruins, blue-blooded artefacts and a gobsmacking library: tiny Slotsholmen packs a powerful punch.

◉ Top Sights

Christiansborg Slot

Explore
Copenhagen

Tivoli Area   22

Slotsholmen   34

Strøget & Around   44

Nyhavn & the Royal Quarter   58

Christianshavn   70

Nørreport   82

Nørrebro   96

Vesterbro   108

Worth a Trip

Østerbro.......................................106
Frederiksburg.................................120
Louisiana Museum of
  Modern Art.................................122

Canalboat dining near Nyhavn (p58)
SARAH COGHILL/LONELY PLANET ©

Explore

Tivoli Area

Copenhagen's veritable welcome mat, the Tivoli area is home to Central Station, the main tourist office and the city's most famous drawcard, Tivoli Gardens. Across the street from the gardens is Rådhuspladsen (City Hall Sq). Dominated by city hall (rådhus), this is the heart of Copenhagen. The square's design is inspired in part by the Palio, the famous piazza in Siena, Italy.

The Sights in a Day

☼ If you're freshly arrived, drop in at the **Copenhagen Visitors Centre** (p151), which offers free wi-fi and a free city map with bus routes. Across the street is the Radisson Blu Royal Hotel, created by Danish design great Arne Jacobsen. From here it's an easy walk to **Rådhus** (p31), Copenhagen's fantastical city hall.

☼ Another quick walk leads you to the **Nationalmuseet** (p28). Spend a few hours nosing through its millennia-spanning collection before lunching at **Kanal Caféen** (p32). Alternatively, lunch in the Winter Garden at **Ny Carlsberg Glyptotek** (p31) before taking in its impressive antiquities and impressionist art.

☾ Trade art for adrenaline across the street at **Tivoli Gardens** (p24). Book a table at vibrant **Gemyse** (p25), one of Tivoli's plethora of eateries. If it's Friday night, catch Tivoli's free summer-season rock concert. Alternatively, snuggle up with a crafty libation at **Nimb Bar** (p33).

👁 Top Sights

Tivoli Gardens (p24)

Nationalmuseet (p28)

💗 Best of Copenhagen

Museums & Galleries

Nationalmuseet (p28)

Ny Carlsberg Glyptotek (p31)

Eating

Restaurant Mes (p32)

Bror (p32)

Kanal Caféen (p32)

For Kids

Tivoli Gardens (p24)

Getting There

🚌 **Bus** Most city routes stop at Central Station or Rådhuspladsen. Routes 6A and 26 reach Frederiksberg Have via Vesterbro. Route 1A reaches Slotsholmen, Nyhavn, the Royal Quarter and Østerbro. Routes 2A and 37 buses reach Christianshavn.

🚆 **S-Train** All S-train lines stop at Central Station and Vesterport. Catch a Helsingør-bound regional train to Humlebæk for Louisiana art museum.

Top Sights
Tivoli Gardens

Unleash your inner child at Tivoli Gardens. This veteran amusement park and pleasure garden has been eliciting gleeful shrills since 1843. It's the world's second-oldest amusement park, and one that inspired none other than Walt Disney. Generations on, the place continues to win fans with its dreamscape of rides, exotic pavilions, concerts, open-air stage shows and fireworks.

👁 Map p30, A3

www.tivoli.dk

adult/child under 8yr 120kr/ free, Fri after 7pm 160kr/free

🕐11am-11pm Sun-Thu, to midnight Fri & Sat early Apr-late Sep, reduced hours rest of year

🚌2A, 5C, 9A, 12, 14, 26, 250S, Ⓢ København H

Star Flyer

One of the world's tallest carousels, the Star Flyer will have you whizzing round and round at heights of up to 80m. It's a bit like being on a skyscraping swing, travelling at 70km/h and taking in a breathtaking view of Copenhagen's historical towers and rooftops. The astrological symbols, quadrants and planets on the ride are a tribute of sorts to Danish astronomer Tycho Brahe.

Roller Coasters

Rutschebanen (The Roller Coaster) is the best loved of Tivoli's roller coasters, rollicking its way through and around a faux 'mountain' and reaching speeds of 60km/h. Built in 1914, it claims to be the world's oldest operating wooden roller coaster. If you're hankering for something a little more hardcore, jump on the Dæmonen (The Demon), a 21st-century beast with faster speeds and a trio of hair-raising loops.

Aquila

Like the Star Flyer, Aquila (Eagle) is also a nod to the country's most famous astronomer; the ride is named for the constellation that Brahe observed through his 16th-century telescope. The attraction itself is a breathtaking, gut-wrenching swing-and-spinner ride, with centrifugal powers up to 4G that will have you spinning around and upside down. If you enjoy viewing the world from a different angle, this one's for you...and your empty stomach.

The Grounds

Beyond the roller coasters, carousels and side stalls is a Tivoli of beautifully landscaped gardens, tranquil nooks and eclectic architecture. Lower the adrenaline under beautiful old

☑ Top Tips

▸ Amusement-ride tickets cost 25kr (some rides require up to three tickets), making the unlimited-ride wristband (230kr) better value if you plan on staying a few hours.

▸ Tivoli is at its most enchanting in the evening.

▸ Although the free Friday music concerts (summer season only) commence at 10pm, head in by 8pm if it's a big-name act or risk missing out.

✗ Take a Break

Fill up on classic Danish fare at **Grøften** (☎33 75 06 75; www.groeften.dk; smørrebrød 79-145kr, mains 149-385kr; ⊙noon-11pm Sun-Thu, to midnight Fri & Sat early Apr-late Sep, reduced hours rest of year; 🛜), Tivoli's most famous dining institution.

For something altogether more sophisticated, opt for **Gemyse** (☎88 70 00 00; www.nimb.dk; 6-course menu 250kr; ⊙noon-11pm; 🛜), also on the grounds.

chestnut and elm trees and amble around Tivoli Lake, gently rippling with koi carps, goldfish and ducks. Formed out of the old city moat, the lake is a top spot to snap pictures of Tivoli's commanding Chinese Tower, built in 1900. The lake itself is also home to the swashbuckling St George III, an 18th-century frigate turned restaurant.

Illuminations & Fireworks

Throughout the summer season, Tivoli Lake wows the crowds with its nightly laser and water spectacular. While it mightn't match the scale of similar shows in cities like Dubai and Las Vegas, its combination of lasers, shooting water and an orchestral score are still entertaining, especially with kids. The best spots to catch the show are from the bridge over Tivoli Lake or in the area in front of the Vertigo ride. Another summer-season must are the Saturday-evening fireworks, repeated again from December 26 to 30 for Tivoli's annual Fireworks Festival. For a good view, make a beeline for Plænen (Tivoli's outdoor stage) or the area around the large fountain. For dates and times, see the website.

Live Performances

Tivoli delivers a jam-packed program of live music. The indoor Tivolis Koncertsal (Concert Hall) hosts mainly classical music, with the odd musical and big-name pop or rock act. Outdoor stage Plænen is the venue for Fredagsrock, Tivoli's free, hugely popular Friday-evening concerts. Running from mid-April to late September, the acts span numerous genres, from pop, rock and neofolk, to hip-hop, jazz and funk (performers have included Lil Wayne, 5 Seconds of Summer and Erykah Badu). All tickets are sold at the Tivoli Billetcenter or online through the Tivoli website.

Christmas Festivities

Even the toughest scrooges find it hard not to melt at the sight of Tivoli in November and December, when the entire park turns into a Yuletide winter wonderland (cue live reindeer and special Christmas rides). The Tivoli Christmas market is one of the city's best-loved traditions, heady with the scent of cookies, pancakes and gløgg (mulled wine). It's also a good spot to pick up some nifty Nordic handicrafts.

Pantomime Theatre

Tivoli's criminally charming Pantomime Theatre debuted in 1874. It's the work of prolific architect Vilhelm Dahlerup, responsible for many of Copenhagen's most iconic buildings, including the Ny Carlsberg Glyptotek and Statens Museum for Kunst. Dahlerup's historicist style shines bright in his Tivoli creation, a colour-bursting ode to the Far East. While plays in the tradition of Italy's Commedia dell'arte are presented here, the stage also plays host to other styles of performances, including modern ballet. See the Tivoli website for details.

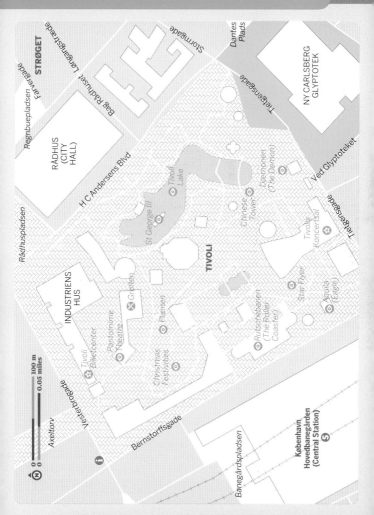

Top Sights
Nationalmuseet

Copenhagen's National Museum hurls visitors through millennia of Danish history. Housed in a former royal palace, it's the country's veritable attic, with a hefty hoard that includes Denmark's fabled Sun Chariot, the well-preserved Huldremose Woman and revealing Viking artefacts. Beyond these weathered Danish icons is an eclectic mix of foreign acquisitions, including classical coins, Chinese robes and Indigenous Australian objects.

National Museum

👁 Map p30, C3

www.natmus.dk

adult/child 75kr/free

🕙10am-5pm Tue-Sun, also open Mon Jul & Aug

🚌1A, 2A, 9A, 14, 26, 37, **S** København H

Danish Prehistory

Many of the museum's most spectacular finds are in the Prehistory Collection, located on the ground floor. Among these is a finely crafted 3500-year-old Sun Chariot and the spectacular Gundestrup cauldron, Europe's oldest example of Iron Age silverwork. Then there's the Huldremose Woman, a well-preserved Iron Age time traveller still wrapped in her cloaks.

Danish Middle Ages & Renaissance

The 1st floor harbours medieval and Renaissance objects from the period 1050 to 1660. Among them are aquamaniles (animal-shaped vessels used in Danish churches for handwashing rituals). The most charming of these is a matching pair, consisting of a young man on horseback and the studiously indifferent woman he is attempting to woo.

Stories of Denmark: 1660-2000

One floor up is the *Stories of Denmark: 1660–2000* exhibition, which traces Denmark's evolution from absolute monarchy to modern nation in three chronological sections: Under the Absolute Monarchy 1660–1848; People and Nation 1848–1915; and Welfare State 1915–2000. Topics include Denmark's string of humiliating wartime defeats, which forced this once powerful, conquering land to reassess its global role.

Ethnographic Treasures

The National Museum's ethnographic collection is one of its lesser-known fortes. Items include an extraordinary child's fur from Canada, fastened with 80 amulets, including fox teeth and a herring gull's foot. Such adornments were believed to ward off evil and lure good fortune.

☑ Top Tips

▶ Tickets are valid all day, allowing you to leave the museum and return later if you feel like breaking up your explorations. Free lockers are available.

▶ The museum has a number of self-guided-tour brochures available for downloading on its website. Among these is a one-hour family tour as well as a children's guide to museum highlights.

✗ Take a Break

Skip the average museum restaurant for a classic Danish feast at nearby, canal-side Kanal Caféen (p32).

For a post-museum vino, kick back at Ved Stranden 10 (p51).

For reviews see	
◉ Top Sights	p24
◉ Sights	p31
✕ Eating	p32
🖰 Drinking	p33
✿ Entertainment	p33

Ny Carlsberg Glyptotek

Sights

Ny Carlsberg Glyptotek   MUSEUM

1 ◎ Map p30, C4

Fin de siècle architecture meets with an eclectic mix of art at Ny Carlsberg Glyptotek. The collection is divided into two parts: Northern Europe's largest booty of antiquities, and an elegant collection of 19th-century Danish and French art. The latter includes the largest collection of Rodin sculptures outside of France and no less than 47 Gauguin paintings. These are displayed along with works by greats like Cézanne, Van Gogh, Pissarro, Monet and Renoir. (☏ 33 41 81 41; www.glyptoteket.dk; Dantes Plads 7, HC Andersens Blvd; adult/child 95kr/free, Tue free; ⏰ 11am-6pm Tue-Sun, until 10pm Thu; ☐ 1A, 2A, 9A, 37, Ⓢ København H)

Rådhus   HISTORIC BUILDING

2 ◎ Map p30, B3

Completed in 1905, Copenhagen's national Romantic-style city hall is the work of architect Martin Nyrop. Inside is the curious **Jens Olsen's World Clock**, designed by astro mechanic Jens Olsen (1872–1945) and built at a cost of one million kroner. It displays not only local time, but also solar time, sidereal time, sunrises and sunsets, firmament and celestial-pole migration, planet revolutions, the Gregorian calendar and even changing

☑️ Top Tip

Many visitors to Ny Carlsberg Glyptotek (p31) miss its wonderful rooftop terrace. Decked out with chairs for lazy lounging, it offers a breathtaking view of the museum's elegant dome, not to mention an impressive view over the city's spire-studded skyline.

holidays! You can also climb the 105m city hall **tower** (30kr; ⊙tour 11am & 2pm Mon-Fri, noon Sat, minimum 4 people) for a commanding view. (City Hall; ☏33 66 25 86; www.kk.dk; Rådhuspladsen; admission free; ⊙9am-4pm Mon-Fri, 9.30am-1pm Sat; 🚌2A, 12, 14, 26, 33, 250S, ⓢKøbenhavn H)

Eating

Restaurant Mes   DANISH $$$

3 🍴 Map p30, A1

This rising star burst onto the Copenhagen dining scene in 2017. Owned by chef Mads Rye Magnusson (former chef at Michelin-three-starred Geranium), it's an intimate, refreshingly whimsical space, complete with moss feature wall and graffiti-soaked restrooms by local artist Fy. The menu is impressive, driven by market produce and the creative whims of its young, highly talented head chef. (☏25 36 51 81; https://restaurant-mes.dk; Jarmers Plads 1; 5-course menu 350kr; ⊙5.30pm-midnight Mon-Sat; 📶; 🚌2A, 5C, 6A, 250S, ⓢVesterport)

Bror   NEW NORDIC $$$

4 🍴 Map p30, B1

Founded by former Noma sous-chefs Sam Nutter and Viktor Wågam, this tiny, split-level bolthole mightn't look like much, but it delivers technically brilliant dishes using superlative Nordic produce. Wines are natural, organic or biodynamic, and expertly paired with beautifully balanced creations like Danish peas with crab meat, crab gel and kombucha, or chocolate mousse with chamomile gel and sorbet, blackberries and tuile. (☏32 17 59 99; www.restaurantbror.dk; Sankt Peders Stræde 24A; 4-/5-course menu 450/625kr; ⊙5.30pm-midnight Wed-Sun; 📶; 🚌2A, 5C, 6A, 250S, ⓜNørreport, ⓢNørreport)

Kanal Caféen   DANISH $$

5 🍴 Map p30, D3

Famed for its gruff staff and excellent herring, this cosy, nautically themed old-timer comes with a shaded summertime pontoon right on the canal. Order some Linie Aquavit (*snaps* matured at sea in oak-sherry casks) and the Kanal Platter, an epic feast of Danish classics, including pickled herring, crumbed plaice, and roast pork with pickled red cabbage. (☏33 11 57 70; www.kanalcafeen.dk; Frederiksholms Kanal 18; smørrebrød 64-127kr; platters per person from 205kr; ⊙11am-5pm Mon-Fri, 11.30am-3pm Sat; 🚌1A, 2A, 9A, 14, 26, 37)

Drinking

Nimb Bar
COCKTAIL BAR

6 | Map p30, A3

If you have a weakness for crystal chandeliers (the originals from 1909), quirky murals and an open fire with your well-mixed drink, make sure this ballroom bar is on your list. Located inside super-chic Hotel Nimb, it was founded by legendary bartender Angus Winchester. The beer is expensive, but you're here for seasonal, classically styled cocktails. Period. (☑88 70 00 00; www.nimb.dk; Hotel Nimb, Bernstorffsgade 5; ☺11am-midnight Sun-Thu, to 1am Fri & Sat; ☂; ☐2A, 5C, 9A, 250S, ⑤København H)

Living Room
CAFE

7 | Map p30, B1

Spread over three levels and decked out in vintage decor and a Moroccan-themed tea room, the aptly titled Living Room is a super-cosy (albeit often busy) spot to settle in with a speciality coffee, tea, homemade smoothie or lemonade. Cocktails and other alcoholic libations are also served late into the evening. (☑33 32 66 10; www.facebook.com/thelivingroomdk; Larsbjørnsstræde 17; ☺9am-11pm Mon-Thu, to 2am Fri, 10am-2am Sat, 10am-7pm Sun; ☂; ☐5C, 6A, 10, 14, Ⓜ Nørreport, ⑤Nørreport)

Local Life

Located inside architect Rem Koolhaas' harbourside Blox building, the Dansk Arkitektur Center (p142) hosts changing exhibitions on Danish and international architecture, and houses an excellent shop. On weekends from late May to September, DAC also runs 90-minute walking tours of the city's contemporary architecture (125kr).

Entertainment

Tivoli Koncertsal
CONCERT VENUE

8 | Map p30, B4

The Tivoli concert hall hosts Danish and international symphony orchestras, string quartets and other performances, not to mention contemporary music artists and dance companies. Purchase tickets online or at the Tivoli Box Office by the main Tivoli Gardens entrance on Vesterbrogade. (www.tivoli.dk; Tietgensgade 30; ☐1A, 2A, 5C, 9A, 37, 250S, ⑤København H)

Mojo
BLUES

9 | Map p30, C3

East of Tivoli, this is a great spot for deep, soulful blues and its associated genres, from bluegrass and zydeco to soul. There are live acts nightly, followed by DJ-spun tunes. The vibe is convivial and relaxed, and there's draught beer aplenty. (☑33 11 64 53; www.mojo.dk; Løngangstræde 21C; ☺8pm-5am; ☐1A, 2A, 9A, 12, 14, 26, 33, 37, ⑤København H)

Explore

Slotsholmen

Slotsholmen is a spire-spiked island heaving with history. At its heart is Christiansborg Slot, home to the national government. Beneath it lie traces of Copenhagen's medieval past, while around it there is an abundance of museums including the Thorvaldsens Museum, an ode to Denmark's greatest sculptor. Adding sharp relief is the Royal Library's 'Black Diamond', one of Scandinavia's most applauded contemporary buildings.

The Sights in a Day

☼ Start the day with a snoop through **Christiansborg Slot** (p36), home to the elegant Royal Reception Rooms and the city's oldest ruins. It will cost you nothing to climb the palace's lofty tower, which offers a commanding view of Denmark's handsome capital.

☼ For a memorable lunch, reserve a table at the tower restaurant, **Tårnet** (p43). Alternatively, keep it simple and cheap with a bite at harbourside cafe **Øieblikket** (p43). The latter sits inside the spectacular 'Black Diamond' building, part of the impressive Det Kongelige Bibliotek.

☾ Once you've finished exploring the library, spend the rest of the day eyeing up the chiselled beauties of Denmark's most revered sculptor at **Thorvaldsens Museum** (p41). Alternatively, learn about a lesser-known part of Danish society at the **Dansk Jødisk Museum** (p42) or inspire your inner thespian at the **Teatermuseet** (p38). Whichever you do choose, don't step off the island without taking a snap of **Børsen** (p42), one of Copenhagen's oldest and most beautiful buildings.

◉ Top Sights

Christiansborg Slot (p36)

♥ Best of Copenhagen

Museums

Thorvaldsens Museum (p41)

Dansk Jødisk Museum (p42)

Ruinerne under Christiansborg (p37)

Architecture

Christiansborg Slot (p36)

Det Kongelige Bibliotek (p41)

Børsen (p42)

Getting There

🚌 **Bus** Slotsholmen is well serviced by bus, with routes 1A, 2A, 9A, 14, 26, 37 and 66 all running across the island. Slotsholmen itself is easily navigable on foot.

Ⓜ **Metro** The closest metro station is Christianshavn, 400m east of Slotsholmen.

⚓ **Boat** Commuter ferries stop just beside Det Kongelige Bibliotek.

Top Sights
Christiansborg Slot

Fans of the Danish political drama *Borgen* will know it as the workplace of *statsminister* Birgitte Nyborg. Others will know it as that slightly foreboding palace in the heart of Copenhagen. This is Denmark's power base, home to the Danish parliament, Prime Minister's office and Supreme Court, not to mention an eclectic array of cultural draws, from tapestries to carriages.

👁 Map p40, B2

www.christiansborg.dk

🕐10am-5pm daily May-Sep, closed Mon Oct-Apr

🚌1A, 2A, 9A, 26, 37, 66
🚤Det Kongelige Bibliotek,
Ⓜ Christianshavn

Royal Reception Rooms, Christiansborg Slot

Royal Reception Rooms

The grandest part of Christiansborg is **De Kongelige Repræsentationslokaler** (Royal Reception Rooms at Christiansborg Slot; adult/child 90kr/free; guided tours in Danish/English 11am/3pm), a series of 18 elegant palace rooms and halls used by the queen to hold royal banquets and entertain heads of state. The Queen's Library is especially memorable, a gilded wonderland adorned with dripping chandeliers, ornate stucco, ceiling storks and a small part of the royal family's centuries-old book collection. Top billing, however, goes to the sweeping Great Hall, home to riotously colourful wall tapestries depicting 1000 years of Danish history. Created by tapestry designer Bjørn Nørgaard over a decade, the works were completed in 2000. Keep an eye out for the Adam and Eve–style representation of the queen and her husband (albeit clothed) in a Danish Garden of Eden.

Fortress Ruins

A walk through the crypt-like bowels of Slotsholmen, known as **Ruinerne under Christiansborg** (Ruins under Christiansborg; adult/child 50kr/free, joint ticket incl royal reception rooms, kitchen & stables 150kr/free), offers a unique perspective on Copenhagen's well-seasoned history. In the basement of the current palace are the ruins of Slotsholmen's original fortress – built by Bishop Absalon in 1167 – and its successor, Copenhagen Castle. Among these remnants are each building's ring walls, as well as a well, baking oven, sewerage drains and stonework from the castle's Blue Tower. The tower is infamously remembered as the place in which Christian IV's daughter, Leonora Christina, was incarcerated for treason from 1663 to 1685.

☑ **Top Tips**

▶ If you plan on visiting several of the sights at Christiansborg Slot, opt for the combination ticket. Costing 150kr (children aged under 18 enter free of charge), it includes access to the Royal Reception Rooms, the Fortress Ruins, the Royal Stables, as well as the surprisingly interesting Royal Kitchen. The ticket is valid for one month.

✕ **Take a Break**

▶ Book a lunch table at Tårnet (p43) for exceptional smørrebrød, beers and a view of Tivoli.

▶ For a cheaper bite, chow down fresh salads and sandwiches by the harbour at Øieblikket (p43).

Royal Stables

Completed in 1740, the two curved, symmetrical wings behind Christiansborg Slot belonged to the original baroque palace, destroyed by fire in 1794. The wings still house De Kongelige Stalde (p42) and its museum of antique coaches, uniforms and riding paraphernalia, some of which are still used for royal receptions. Among these is the 19th-century Gold Coach, adorned with 24-karat gold leaf and used by the royal couple on their gallop from Amalienborg to Christiansborg during the New Year's levee in January.

The Tower

The **palace tower** (https://taarnet.dk; ⊙11am-9pm Tue-Sun) opened to the public for the first time in 2014. It's the city's tallest tower, delivering a sweeping view over the Danish capital. The tower is also home to Tårnet (p43), a restaurant owned by prolific restaurateur Rasmus Bo Bojesen. Lunch features contemporary smørrebrød (open sandwiches) and Danish cheeses; and is a better bet than the dinner, both in terms of value and the view. It's a popular nosh spot, so book ahead if you plan on staking out a table.

Christiansborg Slotskirke

Tragedy struck CF Hansen's austere, 19th-century neoclassical **Christiansborg Slotskirke** (⊙10am-5pm Sun, daily Jul) on the day of the 1992 Copenhagen Carnival. A stray firework hit the scaffolding that had surrounded the church during a lengthy restoration and set the roof ablaze, destroying the dome. With no surviving architectural plans of the dome and roof construction to consult, architectural archaeologists systematically recorded all the charred remains before painstakingly reconstructing the chapel. Miraculously, a remarkable frieze by Bertel Thorvaldsen that rings the ceiling just below the dome survived.

Theatre Museum

Dating from 1767, the wonderfully atmospheric Hofteater (Old Court Theatre) has hosted everything from Italian opera to local ballet troupes, one of which included fledgling ballet student Hans Christian Andersen. Taking its current appearance in 1842, the venue is now the **Teatermuseet** (Theatre Museum; www.teatermuseet.dk; Christiansborg Ridebane 18; adult/child 40kr/free; ⊙noon-4pm Tue-Sun), and visitors are free to explore the stage, boxes and dressing rooms, along with displays of set models, drawings, costumes and period posters tracing the history of Danish theatre.

Understand
Christiansborg Slot's History

Christiansborg Slot is an architectural phoenix. The current palace is simply the latest in a series of buildings to have graced the site, among them medieval castles and an elegant baroque beauty.

Bishop Absalon's Castle
According to medieval chronicler Saxo Grammaticus, Bishop Absalon of Roskilde built a castle on a small islet in the waters off the small town of Havn. The islet would become Slotsholmen. Erected in 1167 the castle was encircled by a limestone curtain wall, the ruins of which can still be seen today under the current complex. Despite frequent attacks, Absalon's creation stood strong for two centuries until a conflict between Valdemar IV of Denmark and the Hanseatic League saw the latter tear it down in 1369.

Copenhagen Castle
By the end of the 14th century, the site was once again thriving, this time as the address of Copenhagen Castle. The new, improved model came with a moat, as well as a solid, towered entrance. The castle remained the property of the Bishop of Roskilde until 1417, when Erik of Pomerania seized control, turning the castle into a royal abode. Nipped and tucked over time – Christian IV added a spire to the entrance tower – the castle was completely rebuilt by Frederik IV, evidently with dubious engineering advice. The castle began to crack under its own weight, leading to its hasty demolition in the 1730s.

Christiansborg: One, Two, Three
The demolition led to the debut of the first Christiansborg Slot in 1745. Commissioned by Christian VI and designed by architect Elias David Häusser, it went up in flames in 1794, its only surviving remnant being the Royal Riding Complex, home to the Royal Stables. Rebuilt in the early 19th century, it became the seat of parliament in 1849 before once more succumbing to fire in 1884. In 1907 the cornerstone for the third Christiansborg Slot was laid by Frederik VIII. Designed by Thorvald Jørgensen and completed in 1928, it's a truly national affair, its neobaroque facade adorned with granite sourced from across the country.

Niels Juels Gade

Christian IV's Bro

Knippelsbro

CHRISTIANSHAVN

Inderhavnen

Holmens Kanal

Nationalbanken

Havnegade

Havnegade

Slotsholms Kanal

Børsen ⊙ **3**

Borsgade

Slotsholmsgade

Christians Brygge

Laksegade

Nikolaigade

Admiralgade

Holmens Bro

Ministerialbygning

Søren Kierkegaards ⊗ **8**
Plads

Ved Stranden

Christiansborg
Slotsplads

Tøjhusgade

Dansk
Jødisk ⊙ **4**
Museum

Det Kongelige Biblioteks Have

Det Kongelige
Bibliotek ⊙ **2**

⊗ **9**

Højbro

⊗ **7**

Vindebrogade

⊙ **Christiansborg
Slot**

Tøjhusmuseet ⊙ **6**

SLOTSHOLMEN

Christian IV's
Bryghus

Bertel ⊙ **1 Thorvaldsens**
Thorvaldsens Museum
Plads

Christiansborg
Ridebane

De Kongelige
Stalde **5** ⊙

Prinsensbro

Frederiksholms Kanal

Porthusgade

Marmorbroen

Frederiksholms Kanal

Slotsholmens Kanal

Stormbro

Nationalmuseet

Ny Vestergade

Ny Kongensgade

Snaregade

Magstræde

Knabrostræde

Nybrogade

100 m
0.05 miles

	For reviews see	
⊙	Top Sights	p36
⊙	Sights	p41
⊗	Eating	p43

JOHNER IMAGES/GETTY IMAGES ©

Black Diamond

Sights

Thorvaldsens Museum MUSEUM

1 ◉ Map p40, B1

What looks like a colourful Greco-Roman mausoleum is in fact a museum dedicated to the works of illustrious Danish sculptor Bertel Thorvaldsen (1770–1844). Heavily influenced by mythology after four decades in Rome, Thorvaldsen returned to Copenhagen and donated his private collection to the Danish public. In return the royal family provided this site for the construction of what is a remarkable complex housing Thorvaldsen's drawings, plaster moulds and statues. The museum also contains Thorvaldsen's own collection of Mediterranean antiquities. (☏33 32 15 32; www.thorvaldsens museum.dk; Bertel Thorvaldsens Plads 2; adult/child 70kr/free, Wed free; ⏱10am-5pm Tue-Sun; ☒1A, 2A, 26, 37, 66)

Det Kongelige Bibliotek LIBRARY

2 ◉ Map p40, C4

Scandinavia's largest library consists of two very distinct parts: the original 19th-century red-brick building and the head-turning 'Black Diamond' extension, the latter a leaning parallelogram of sleek black granite and smoke-coloured glass. From the soaring, harbour-fronting atrium, an escalator leads up to a 210 sq metre ceiling mural by celebrated Danish

☑ Top Tip

Music at One

If possible, drop into the Black Diamond at the Royal Library (p41) at 1pm, when the usually quiet space breaks into a dramatic three-minute soundscape. Created by Danish composer Jens Vilhelm Pedersen (aka Fuzzy) and titled *Katalog* (Catalogue), the work consists of 52 individual electro-acoustic compositions, one for each week of the year.

artist Per Kirkeby. Beyond it, at the end of the corridor, is the 'old library' and its Hogwarts-like northern Reading Room, resplendent with vintage desk lamps and classical columns. (Royal Library; 📞 33 47 47 47; www.kb.dk; Søren Kierkegaards Plads; admission free; ⏱ 8am-7pm Mon-Fri, from 9am Sat Jul & Aug, 8am-9pm Mon-Fri, 9am-7pm Sat rest of year; 🚌 66, 🚇 Det Kongelige Bibliotek)

Børsen
HISTORIC BUILDING

3 ◎ Map p40, D2

Not many stock exchanges are topped by a 56m-tall spire formed from the entwined tails of four dragons. Børsen is one. Constructed in the bustling early-17th-century reign of Christian IV, the building is considered one of the finest examples of Dutch Renaissance architecture in Denmark, with richly embellished gables. Its still-functioning chamber of commerce is the oldest in Europe, though the

building is not generally open to the public. (Børsgade; 🚌 2A, 9A, 37, 66)

Dansk Jødisk Museum
MUSEUM

4 ◎ Map p40, C3

Designed by Polish-born Daniel Libeskind, the Danish Jewish Museum occupies the former Royal Boat House, an early 17th-century building once part of Christian IV's harbour complex. The transformed interior is an intriguing geometrical space, home to a permanent exhibition documenting Danish Jewry. Historical events covered include the Rescue of the Danish Jews in WWII, in which most of the country's Jewish population managed to flee to neutral Sweden with the help of the Danish resistance movement and ordinary Danish citizens. (📞 33 11 22 18; www.jewmus.dk; Proviantpassagen 6, Kongelige Bibliotekshave (Royal Library Garden); adult/child 60kr/free; ⏱ 10am-5pm Tue-Sun Jun-Aug, 1-4pm Tue-Fri, noon-5pm Sat & Sun rest of the year; 🚌 66, 🚇 Det Kongelige Bibliotek)

De Kongelige Stalde
MUSEUM

5 ◎ Map p40, B3

Completed in 1740, the two curved, symmetrical wings behind Christiansborg belonged to the original baroque palace, destroyed by fire in 1794. The wings still house the royal stables and its museum of antique coaches, uniforms and riding paraphernalia, some of which are still used for royal receptions. Among these is the 19th-century Gold Coach, adorned with 24-carat gold leaf and still used by the queen on her gallop from Amalienborg to Christiansborg during the New Year's levee in January. (Royal Stables; ☎33 40 10 10; www.kongehuset.dk; adult/child 50kr/free; ⏱1.30-4pm daily May-Sep, closed Mon Oct-Apr, guided tours in English 2pm Sat; 🚌1A, 2A, 9A, 26, 37, 66)

Tøjhusmuseet   MUSEUM

6 ◉ Map p40, B3

The Royal Arsenal Museum houses an impressive collection of historic weaponry, from canons and medieval armour to pistols, swords and even a WWII flying bomb. Built by Christian IV in 1600, the 163m-long building is Europe's longest vaulted Renaissance hall. (Royal Danish Arsenal Museum; ☎33 11 60 37; www.natmus.dk; Tøjhusgade 3; adult/child 65kr/free; ⏱10am-5pm Tue-Sun; 🚌1A, 2A, 9A, 14, 26, 37, 66)

Eating

Tårnet   DANISH $$

7 ✕ Map p40, C2

Book ahead for lunch at Tårnet, owned by prolific restaurateur Rasmus Bo Bojesen and memorably set inside Christiansborg Slot's commanding tower. Lunch here is better value than dinner, with superlative, contemporary smørrebrød that is among the city's best. While the general guideline is two smørrebrød per person, some of the a la carte versions are quite substantial (especially the tartare), so check before ordering. (☎33 37 31 00; http://taarnet.dk/restauranten;

Christiansborg Slotsplads, Christiansborg Slot; lunch smørrebrød 85-135kr, dinner mains 235kr; ⏱11.30am-11pm Tue-Sun, kitchen closes 10pm; 🛜; 🚌1A, 2A, 9A, 26, 37, 66; Ⓜ Det Kongelige Bibliotek)

Søren K   NEW NORDIC $$$

8 ✕ Map p40, D4

Bathed in light on even the dourest of days, the Royal Library's crisp, harbourfront fine-diner revels in flaunting top-notch, seasonal ingredients. The menu focuses on small plates, each delivering delicate, contemporary takes on mainly Nordic flavours, whether it be raw scallop with salted cucumber and green tomato bouillon, or Norwegian lobster with anchovy and kale. Come for the quality, not the portions. (☎33 47 49 49; http://soerenk.dk; Søren Kierkegaards Plads 1; 1/5 courses 120/500kr; ⏱noon-3pm & 5.30-10pm Mon-Sat; 🛜; 🚌66, Ⓜ Det Kongelige Bibliotek)

Øieblikket   CAFE $

9 ✕ Map p40, C4

The Royal Library's ground-floor cafe delivers a short menu of cheap, fresh bites, with one soup, a couple of salads and sandwiches, and no shortage of naughty cakes and pastries for a mid-afternoon high. The coffee is acceptable and the harbourside deckchairs are a top spot to soak up some rays on those sunny summer afternoons. (☎33 47 41 06; Søren Kierkegaards Plads 1; soup & salads 40-45kr, sandwiches 50-55kr; ⏱8am-7pm Mon-Fri, 9am-6pm Sat; 🛜🍴; 🚌9A, Ⓜ Det Kongelige Bibliotek)

Explore

Strøget & Around

Pedestrianised Strøget (pronounced 'stroll') weaves through Co-penhagen's historical core from Rådhuspladsen to Kongens Nytorv. Many of the most interesting sights, restaurants, bars and boutiques, however, lie off the main drag, in or around the old Latin Quarter. Among them is Copenhagen's austere, sculpture-graced cathedral and King Christian IV's curious 17th-century Round Tower.

The Sights in a Day

☀️ Begin in the **Latin Quarter** (p48), taking in Bertel Thorvaldsen's sculptures inside **Vor Frue Kirke** (p48) and exploring the bookshops, cafes, boutiques and centuries-old architecture on streets like Studiestræde, Krystalgade, Fiolstræde and Kannikestræde. At the eastern end of Kannikestræde stands **Rundetårn** (p48), worth climbing for the view.

☀️ Combine history and smørrebrød (open sandwiches) at local institution **Schønnemann** (p50). Alternatively, chow an organic hot dog at **DØP** (p51); a vegetarian version is available. The streets east of DØP and Schønnemann are packed with inspired shops, including homegrown **Han Kjøbenhavn** (p57), **Wood Wood** (p57), and **Hay House** (p55). Alternatively, opt for an afternoon of contemporary art at **Kunstforeningen GL Strand** (p48) and **Nikolaj Kunsthal** (p49).

🌙 Sip well-picked vino at **Ved Stranden 10** (p51) or gorgeous cocktails at **Ruby** (p52), then dine at pan-Asian hotspot **The Market** (p50) or reserve a table at New-Nordic **Marv & Ben** (p50). If it's not early in the week, cap the evening with drinks at **1105** (p52).

💜 **Best of Stroget & Around**

Eating
Schønnemann (p50)

The Market (p50)

Drinking
Ved Stranden 10 (p51)

Ruby (p52)

Mother Wine (p52)

Shopping
Hay House (p55)

Stilleben (p55)

Storm (p56)

Posterland (p56)

Getting There

🚌 **Bus** Most major routes skirt the compact historic centre. The only route that actually traverses it is route 14, connecting Nørreport to Vesterbro via Tivoli Gardens and Central Station.

Ⓜ **Metro** Kongens Nytorv station is just off the eastern end of Stroget. At the northwest edge of the city centre lies Nørreport station, serving both the metro and S-train.

For reviews see

⊙ Sights	p48
⊗ Eating	p50
☻ Drinking	p51
☆ Entertainment	p53
🔒 Shopping	p55

A **B** **C** **D**

Ⓜ Nørreport

Nørreport
Ⓢ

Frederiksborggade

Rosenborggade

Hausergad

Kultorve

Rømersgade

Vendersgade

Israels
Plads

Linnésgade

Rosengården

Peder

Hvitfeldts Stræde

Nansensgade

Nørre Voldgade

Nørregade

Fiolstræde

Krystalgade

1 ⊙ ☻ **16**

Latin
Quarter

Kannikestræde

Klosterstræ

Ørsteds
Parken

Nørre Farimagsgade

Larslejsstræde

Teglgårdsstræde

Københavns
Universitet

Vor Frue Plads

Fiolstræde

⊙ **3**

Vor Frue Kirke

Skoubogade

Skindergade

11 ⊗

Gammeltorv

Nygade

Knabrostræde

Nørre Voldgade

Sankt Pedersstræde

Larsbjørnsstræde

Studiestræde

Nytorv

Brolæggerstræ

Hammerichsgade

Studiestræde

Vester Voldgade

Vestergade

Frederiksberggade (Strøget)

Kattesundet

Slutterigade

Knabrostræde

H C Andersens Blvd

Lavendelstræde

Hestemøllestræde

Farvergade

Kompagnistræde

Rådhusstræ

Rådhuspladsen
Ⓜ **(under
construction)**

Rådhuspladsen

Regnbuepladsen

Løngangstræde

Jernbanegade

Axeltorv

Vesterbrogade

Tivoli

Rådhus
(City Hall)

NØRREPORT

Kongens
Have

Gothersgade

Åbenrå
Hauser
Plads ⊗7
ustervig

Landemærket

Rundetårn
2⊙⊗10
Købmagergade

ndergade

Niels Hemmingsensgade

åbrødretorv

❸18

20❶
Vimmelskaftet
6⊙
Strædet
Hyskenstræde
Læderstræde

Kunstforeningen
GL Strand
8⊗ 4⊙
Snaregade
Gammel Strand
Slotsholms Kanal
⊙13
Magstræde
brogade
Porthusgade
Stormbro

SLOTSHOLMEN

Kronprinsessegade

Adelgade

Landgreven

Dronningens
Tværgade

Store Kongensgade

Borgergade

Ny Adelgade

Gothersgade

Lønporten

Vognmagergade
Sjæleboderne

Møntergade

25❶
Ny Østergade

17⊙

22

27

23❶❶

Grønnegade

Hovedvagtsgade

Kongens
Nytorv

Klareboderne

Gammel Mønt

Sværtegade

Kronprinsensgade

14❷

26❶
24

Antonigade
9⊗

❶15

Kristen
Berikows Gade

Silkegade
Pilestræde

21❶
19❶
Østergade
Store Kirkestræde

Østergade

Lille Kongensgade

Charlottenborg

**Kongens
Nytorv**

Holmens
Kanal

Vingårdsstræde

Amagertorv

Gammel
Strand (under
construction)

Højbro Plads
⊙Nikolaj
5 Kunsthal

Fortunstræde

Dybens Gade

Bremerholm

Tordenskjoldsgade

Niels Juels Gade

Gammel Strand
Højbro
Vindebrogade

Boldhusgade
12❶
Ved Stranden

Laksegade

Nikolajgade

Admiralgade

Laksegade

Holmens Kanal

Holmens
Bro

Holmens
Kanal

Nationalbanken

Havnegade

Christiansborg Slot

Tøjhusgade

Slotsholmsgade

Børsbroen

Børsgade

⊗N 0 _____ 200 m
0 _____ 0.1 miles

Sights

Latin Quarter
AREA

1 ⊙ Map p46, D2

Bordered by Nørre Voldgade to the north, Nørregade to the east, Vestergade to the south and Vester Voldgade to the west, the Latin Quarter gets its nickname from the presence of the old campus of **Københavns Universitet** (Copenhagen University), where Latin was once widely spoken. This is one of Copenhagen's oldest and most atmospheric districts, dotted with historic, pastel-hued buildings and postcard-pretty nooks. Among the latter is **Gråbrødretorv** (Grey Friars' Square), which dates from the mid-17th century. (⊡5C, 6A, 14, MNørreport, SNørreport)

Rundetårn
HISTORIC BUILDING

2 ⊙ Map p46, E2

Haul yourself to the top of the 34.8m-high red-brick 'Round Tower' and you will be following in the footsteps of such luminaries as King Christian IV, who built it in 1642 as an observatory for the famous astronomer Tycho Brahe. You'll also be following in the hoofsteps of Tsar Peter the Great's horse and, according to legend, the track marks of a car that made its way up the tower's spiral ramp in 1902. (Round Tower; ☎33 73 03 73; www.rundetaarn.dk; Købmagergade 52; adult/child 25/5kr; ☉10am-8pm May-Sep, reduced hours rest of year, observatory times vary; ⊡14, MNørreport, SNørreport)

Vor Frue Kirke
CATHEDRAL

3 ⊙ Map p46, D3

Founded in 1191 and rebuilt three times after devastating fires, Copenhagen's neoclassical cathedral dates from 1829. Designed by CF Hansen, its lofty, vaulted interior houses Bertel Thorvaldsen's statues of Christ and the apostles, completed in 1839 and considered his most acclaimed works. In fact, the sculptor's depiction of Christ, with comforting open arms, remains the most popular world-wide model for statues of Jesus. In May 2004, the cathedral hosted the wedding of Crown Prince Frederik to Australian Mary Donaldson. (☎33 15 10 78; www.koebenhavnsdomkirke.dk; Nørregade 8; ☉8am-5pm, closed during services & concerts; ⊡14, MNørreport, SNørreport)

Kunstforeningen GL Strand
GALLERY

4 ⊙ Map p46, E4

The HQ of Denmark's artists' union continues to foster emerging and forward-thinking talent with around six to eight exhibitions of modern and contemporary art each year. The work of both Danish and international artists is explored, with an underlying emphasis on current and emerging trends in the art world. That said, retrospectives are also occasionally offered; a recent exhibition showcased the work of Finnish illustrator and writer Tove Jansson, creator of the much-loved Moomins storybook characters. (☎33 36 02 60; www.glstrand.dk;

Christ Statue, Vor Frue Kirke

Gammel Strand 48; adult/child 75kr/free; ⏱11am-5pm Tue & Thu-Sun, to 8pm Wed; 🚌1A, 2A, 9A, 26, 37, 66, Ⓜ Kongens Nytorv)

Nikolaj Kunsthal
GALLERY

5 ◎ Map p46, G4

Built in the 13th century, the church of Sankt Nikolaj is now home to the **Copenhagen Contemporary Art Centre**, which hosts around half-a-dozen exhibitions annually. Exhibitions tend to focus on modern-day cultural, political and social issues, explored in mediums as diverse as photography and performance art. The centre also houses a snug, well-regarded Danish restaurant called **Maven**. (📞33 18 17 80; www.nikolaj

kunsthal.dk; Nikolaj Plads 10; adult/child 60kr/free, Wed free; ⏱noon-6pm Tue-Fri, 11am-5pm Sat & Sun; 🚌1A, 2A, 9A, 26, 37, 66, 350S, Ⓜ Kongens Nytorv)

Strædet
STREET

6 ◎ Map p46, E4

Running parallel to crowded Strøget, Strædet is technically made up of two streets, Kompagnistræde and Læderstræde. The strip is a good spot to shop for local ceramics and antiques, though its cafes are mostly mediocre. Many of Strædet's medieval and Renaissance-era buildings were destroyed in the great fire of 1795, though some do survive. These include the buildings at numbers 23,

25, 31 and 33, all of which date back to the first half of the 1700s. (🖵1A, 2A,9A, 14, 26, 37, 66)

Eating

Schønnemann   DANISH $$

7 ✕ Map p46, E1

A veritable institution, Schønnemann has been lining bellies with smørrebrød and snaps since 1877. Originally a hit with farmers in town selling their produce, the restaurant's current fan base includes revered chefs like René Redzepi; try the smørrebrød named after him: smoked halibut with creamed cucumber, radishes and chives on caraway bread. (📞33 12 07 85; www.restaurantschonnemann.dk; Hauser Plads 16; smørrebrød 75-185kr; ⏱11.30am-5pm Mon-Sat; 📶; 🖵6A, 42, 150S, 184, 185, 350S, Ⓜ Nørreport, Ⓢ Nørreport)

Marv & Ben   NEW NORDIC $$$

8 ✕ Map p46, E4

Cellar restaurant 'Marrow & Bone' has been repeatedly awarded a Michelin Bib Gourmand in recognition of its value for money. Its New Nordic menu can be approached in various ways: a la carte or as four- or six-course tasting menus. Dishes are imaginative and evocative, celebrating Nordic landscapes and moods in creations like hay-smoked mackerel with chamomile or squid with kelp and buttermilk. (📞33 91 01 91; www.marvog ben.dk; Snaregade 4; small dishes 85-135kr, 4/6-course menu 400/600kr; ⏱5.30pm-1am Tue-Sat; 📶; 🖵1A, 2A, 9A, 14, 26, 37)

The Market   ASIAN $$

9 ✕ Map p46, F3

Dark, svelte and contemporary (we love the dramatically back-lit bar and organically shaped crockery), The Market pumps out vibrant pan-Asian dishes like delicate brown-crab salad with apple, dashi and avocado, or expertly grilled poussin dressed in coconut sauce and fresh mango slithers. The sushi is commendable, particularly the maki. Book ahead, especially if dining on a Friday or Saturday night. (📞70 70 24 35; http://themarketcph. dk; Antongade 2; mains 155-350kr, 12-course menu 595kr; ⏱11.30am-4pm & 5-10pm Mon-

---

☑ Top Tip

Smart Bikes

Copenhagen's bike-share program is called **Bycyklen** (City Bikes; www. bycyklen.dk; per 1hr 30kr). Available 24/7, 365 days a year, these 'Smart Bikes' feature touchscreen tablets with GPS, electric motors, puncture-resistant tyres and locks. The bikes can be accessed from a large number of docking stations dotted across the city, including at Central Station, Vesterport, Østerport and Dybbølsbro S-train stations. To use, you will first need to create an account on the Bycyklen website. Check the website for docking stations locations and real-time bicycle availability at each. Rental itself costs 30kr per hour.

Thu, to 10.30am Fri & Sat, to 9.30pm Sun; 🚌1A, 26, Ⓜ️Kongens Nytorv)

DØP

HOT DOGS $

10 🍴 Map p46, E2

Danes love a good *pølse* (sausage), and hot-dog vans are ubiquitous across Copenhagen. DØP is the best, with a van right beside Rundetårn (Round Tower). Everything here is organic, from the meat and vegetables to the toppings. Options range from a classic Danish roasted hot dog with mustard, ketchup, remoulade, pickles and onions both fresh and fried, to a new-school vegan tofu version. (🖉30 20 40 25; www.døp.dk; Købmagergade 50; hot dogs from 35kr; ⏰11am-6.30pm Mon-Sat; 🚌14, Ⓜ️Nørrebro, Ⓢ️Nørrebro)

La Glace

BAKERY $

11 🍴 Map p46, D4

Copenhagen's oldest *konditori* (pastry shop) has been compromising waistlines since 1870. Slip into its maze of time-warped rooms and succumb to a slice of the classic *valnøddekage* (walnut cake), a cheeky combo of crushed and caramelised walnuts, whipped cream and mocca glacé. If you're a marzipan lover, opt for the chocolate-covered Dachstein; its moist, flavourful centre is good enough to leave you purring. (🖉33 14 46 46; www.laglace.dk; Skoubogade 3; cake slices 57kr, pastries from 36kr; ⏰8.30am-6pm Mon-Fri, 9am-6pm Sat, 10am-6pm Sun; 🛜♿; 🚌14)

Local Life

Cosy, creaky, wood-panelled **Café Halvvejen** (Map p46, D2; 🖉33 11 91 12; www.cafehalvvejen.dk; Krystalgade 11; dishes 55-125kr; ⏰11am-2am Mon-Thu, to 3am Fri & Sat; 🚌5A, 6A, 14, 150S, Ⓜ️Nørreport, Ⓢ️Nørreport) channels a fast-fading Copenhagen. The menu is unapologetically hearty, generous and cheap for this part of town, with faithful open sandwiches, *frikadeller* (Danish meatballs) and *pariserbøf* (minced beef steak with egg and onions). The deceptively named *mini-platte* offers a satisfying overview of classic Nordic flavours. Whatever you choose, wash it down with a (very generous) shot of akvavit.

Drinking

Ved Stranden 10

WINE BAR

12 🍷 Map p46, F4

Politicians and well-versed oenophiles make a beeline for this canal-side wine bar, its enviable cellar stocked with classic European vintages, biodynamic wines and more obscure drops. With modernist Danish design and friendly, clued-in staff, its string of rooms lend an intimate, civilised air that's perfect for grown-up conversation. Discuss terroir and tannins over vino-friendly nibbles like olives, cheeses and smoked meats. (🖉35 42 40 40; www.vedstranden10.dk; Ved Stranden 10; ⏰noon-10pm Mon-Sat; 🛜; 🚌1A, 2A, 9A, 26, 37, 66, 350S, Ⓜ️Kongens Nytorv)

Q **Local Life**

Board Games & Beer

A godsend on rainy days, hugely popular, supercosy **Bastard Café** (Map p46,D5; ☑42 74 66 42; https://bas tardcafe.dk; Rådhusstræde 13; ⏰noon-midnight Sun-Thu, to 2am Fri & Sat; 🚌1A, 2A, 9A, 14, 26, 37) is dedicated to board games, which line its rooms like books in a library. Some are free to use, while others incur a small 'rental fee'. While away the hours playing an old favourite or learn the rules of a more obscure option.

Ruby
COCKTAIL BAR

13 🚇 Map p46, E5

Cocktail connoisseurs raise their glasses to high-achieving Ruby, hidden away in an unmarked 18th-century townhouse. Inside, suave mixologists whip up near-flawless, seasonal libations created with craft spirits and homemade syrups, while a lively crowd spills into a labyrinth of cosy, decadent rooms. For a gentlemen's club vibe, head downstairs among chesterfields, oil paintings and wooden cabinets lined with spirits. (☑33 93 12 03; www.rby.dk; Nybrogade 10; ⏰4pm-2am Mon-Sat, from 6pm Sun; 📶; 🚌1A, 2A, 14, 26, 37, 66)

Mother Wine
WINE BAR

14 🚇 Map p46, F2

A *hyggelig* (cosy) wine bar/shop with some very prized Finn Juhl chairs, Mother Wine showcases natural, organic and lesser-known Italian drops. From organic Veneto Prosecco to Puglian Negroamaro, guests are encouraged to sample the day's rotating offerings before committing to a glass. Wines start at a very palatable 55kr and come with a small complimentary serve of Italian nibbles. (☑33 12 10 00; http://motherwine.dk; Gammel Mønt 33; ⏰10am-7pm Mon-Wed, to 10pm Thu & Sat, to late Fri; 📶; 🚌350S, Ⓜ Kongens Nytorv)

1105
COCKTAIL BAR

15 🚇 Map p46, G3

Head in before 11pm for a bar seat at this dark, luxe lounge. Named for the local postcode, its cocktail repertoire spans both the classic and the revisited. You'll also find a fine collection of whiskeys, not to mention an older 30- and 40-something crowd more interested in thoughtfully crafted drinks than partying hard and getting wasted. (☑33 93 11 05; www.1105. dk; Kristen Bernikows Gade 4; ⏰8pm-2am Wed, Thu & Sat, 4pm-2am Fri; 🚌1A, 26, 350S, Ⓜ Kongens Nytorv)

Democratic Coffee
COFFEE

16 🚇 Map p46, D3

Democratic Coffee is not your typical library coffee shop, and it's not just for students: it's popular with locals and tourists alike. The long wooden coffee bar offers espresso as well as V60-brewed coffee, and the freshly baked croissants (20kr) have been called the best in the city, especially the popular almond variety. (Watch your clothes:

Ruby bar

the filling is rich and runny.) (📞40 19 62 37; Krystalgade 15; ⏰8am-7pm Mon-Fri, 9am-4pm Sat; 📶; 🚌14, Ⓜ Nørreport, Ⓢ Nørreport)

Entertainment

Jazzhus Montmartre JAZZ

17 ⭐ Map p46, G2

Saxing things up since the late 1950s, this is one of Scandinavia's great jazz venues, with past performers including Dexter Gordon, Ben Webster and Kenny Drew. Today, it continues to host local and international talent. On concert nights, you can also tuck into a decent, three-course set menu (375kr) at the cafe-restaurant.

(📞70 26 32 67; www.jazzhusmontmartre.dk; Store Regnegade 19A; ⏰6pm-midnight Thu-Sat; 🚌350S, 1A, 26, Ⓜ Kongens Nytorv)

Jazzhouse JAZZ

18 ⭐ Map p46, E3

One of Copenhagen's leading jazz joints, Jazzhouse hosts top Danish and visiting talent, with music styles running the gamut from bebop to fusion jazz. On weekdays, concerts usually start at 8pm, on Friday and Saturday, acts normally hit the stage around 9pm. Check the website for upcoming acts, times and prices. (📞33 15 47 00; www.jazzhouse.dk; Niels Hemmingsensgade 10; ⏰from 7pm Mon-Thu, from 8pm Fri-Sat; 📶; 🚌1A, 2A, 9A, 14, 26, 37)

Understand
Danish Design

Visit a Copenhagen home and you'll invariably find Poul Henningsen lamps hanging from the ceiling, Arne Jacobsen or Hans Wegner chairs in the dining room, and the table set with Royal Copenhagen dinner sets, Stelton cutlery and Bodum glassware. Here, good design is not just for museums and institutions: it's an integral part of daily life.

Iconic Chairs

Modern Danish furniture is driven by the principle that design should be tailored to the comfort of the user – a principle most obvious in Denmark's world-famous designer chairs. Among the classics is Hans Wegner's Round Chair (1949). Proclaimed 'the world's most beautiful chair' by US *Interiors* magazine in 1950, it would find fame as the chair used by Nixon and Kennedy in their televised presidential debates in 1960. The creations of modernist architect Arne Jacobsen are no less iconic. Designed for Copenhagen's Radisson Blu Royal Hotel, the Egg Chair (1958) is the essence of jet-setting midcentury modernity. His revolutionary Ant Chair (1952), the model for stacking chairs found in schools and cafeterias worldwide, found infamy as the chair on which callgirl Christine Keeler (from the British Profumo Affair) sat in a 1960s Lewis Morley photograph.

Switched-on Lighting

Danish design prevails in stylish lamps as well. The country's best-known lamp designer was Poul Henningsen (1894–1967), who emphasised the need for lighting to be soft, for the shade to cast a pleasant shadow and for the light bulb to be blocked from direct view. His PH5 lamp (1958) remains one of the most popular hanging lamps sold in Denmark today. The popularity of fellow modernist designer Verner Panton is no less enduring. Like Henningsen, Panton was interested in creating lighting that hid the light source, a goal achieved to playful effect with his signature Flowerpot lamp (1968). The designer, who worked for Arne Jacobsen's architectural office from 1950 to 1952, would also go down as an innovative furniture designer, his plastic single-piece Panton Chair (1967) one of the 20th century's most famous furniture pieces.

Shopping

Hay House
DESIGN

19 🔒 Map p46, F3

Rolf Hay's fabulous interior-design store sells its own coveted line of furniture, textiles and design objects, as well as those of other fresh, innovative Danish designers. Easy-to-pack gifts include anything from notebooks and ceramic cups, to building blocks for style-savvy kids. There's a second branch at Pilestræde 29-31. (📞 42 82 08 20; www.hay.dk; Østergade 61; ⏰ 10am-6pm Mon-Fri, to 5pm Sat; 🚌 1A, 2A, 9A, 14, 26, 37, 66, Ⓜ Kongens Nytorv)

Stilleben
DESIGN

20 🔒 Map p46, E3

Owned by Danish Design School graduates Ditte Reckweg and Jelena Schou Nordentoft, Stilleben stocks a bewitching range of contemporary ceramic, glassware, jewellery and textiles from mostly emerging Danish and foreign designers. Head up the wooden stairs for posters and prints, including works by celebrated contemporary Danish artist Cathrine Raben Davidsen. There's a second branch opposite gourmet-food market Torvehallerne KBH. (📞 33 91 11 31; www.stilleben.dk; Niels Hemmingsensgade 3; ⏰ 10am-6pm Mon-Fri, to 5pm Sat; 🚌 1A, 2A, 9A, 14, 26, 37, 66, Ⓜ Kongens Nytorv)

Illums Bolighus
DESIGN

21 🔒 Map p46, F3

Design fans hyperventilate over this sprawling department store, its four floors packed with all things Nordic and beautiful. You'll find everything from ceramics, glassware, jewellery and fashion to throws, lamps, furniture and more. It's also a handy spot to pick up some X-factor souvenirs, from posters, postcards and notebooks adorned with vintage Danish graphics to design-literate Danish wallets and key rings. (📞 33 14 19 41; www.illumsbolighus.dk; Amagertorv 8-10; ⏰ 10am-7pm Mon-Thu & Sat, to 8pm Fri, 11am-5pm Sun; 📶; 🚌 1A, 2A, 9A, 14, 26, 37, 66, Ⓜ Kongens Nytorv)

Q Local Life

Cinemateket

Cinephiles flock to the Danish Film Institute's **Cinemateket** (Map p47, F1; 📞 33 74 34 12; www.dfi.dk; Gothersgade 55; ⏰ 9.30am-10pm Tue-Fri, noon-10pm Sat, noon-7.30pm Sun; 🚌 350S), which screens around 70 films per month, including twice-monthly classic Danish hits (with English subtitles) on Sundays. The centre also houses an extensive library of film and TV literature, a 'videotheque' with more than 1500 titles – including feature films, shorts, documentaries and TV series – as well as a shop and restaurant-cafe.

Storm
FASHION & ACCESSORIES

22 🔒 Map p46, F2

Storm is one of Copenhagen's most inspired fashion pit stops, with trend-setting men's and women's labels such as Haider Ackermann, Kitsuné and Thom Browne. The vibe is youthful and street smart, with extras including statement sneakers, boutique fragrances, art and design tomes, fashion magazines and jewellery. Obligatory for the cashed-up, street-smart style crew. (🖉 33 93 00 14; www.stormfashion.dk; Store Regnegade 1; ⏰11am-5.30pm Mon-Thu, to 7pm Fri, 10am-4pm Sat; 🚌1A, 26, 350S, Ⓜ Kongens Nytorv)

NN07
FASHION & ACCESSORIES

23 🔒 Map p46, F2

This is the striking flagship store for Danish menswear brand NN07 (aka: No Nationality). The threads here are understated and contemporary, ranging from soft jersey tees and street-smart sweat tops, to stylish knits, crisp-collared shirts and chinos in easy-to-match block colours. These goods aren't cheap, but the quality is high and the pieces are designed to last. Accessories include leather belts and bags. (🖉 38 41 11 41; www.nn07.com; Gammel Mønt 7; ⏰10am-6pm Mon-Thu, to 7pm Fri, to 5pm Sat, noon-4pm Sun; 🚌1A, 26, 350S, Ⓜ Kongens Nytorv)

Baum und Pferdgarten
FASHION & ACCESSORIES

24 🔒 Map p46, F2

Designers Rikke Baumgarten and Helle Hestehave are the creative forces behind what is one of Denmark's most respected women's fashion brands. While there's no shortage of pared-back Copenhagen chic, the collections here always fuse a sense of quirkiness, fun and subversiveness. Expect sharp, structured silhouettes, playful prints and beautiful fabrics. (🖉35 30 10 90; www.baumundpferdgarten.com; Vognmagergade 2; ⏰10am-6pm Mon-Thu, to 7pm Fri, to 5pm Sat; 🚌350S, Ⓜ Kongens Nytorv)

Posterland
GIFTS & SOUVENIRS

25 🔒 Map p46, F2

Posterland is Northern Europe's biggest poster company and the main art supplier for the gallery shops of the National Gallery of Denmark and the Louisiana Museum of Modern Art. Spruce up your walls with art, travel and vintage posters, as well Copenhagen-themed posters showcasing iconic locations like Tivoli Gardens and the Carlsberg Brewery. (🖉33 11 28 21; www.posterland.dk; Gothersgade 45; ⏰9.30am-6pm Mon-Thu, to 7pm Fri, to 5pm Sat; 🚌350S, Ⓜ Kongens Nytorv)

Illums Bolighus (p55)

Han Kjøbenhavn
FASHION & ACCESSORIES

26 Map p46, F2

While we love the uncluttered Modernist fit-out, it's what's on the racks that will hook you: simple, beautifully crafted men's threads that merge Scandinavian sophistication with street smarts and a hint of old-school Danish working-class culture. The label has often collaborated with other designers, like Australian shoemaker Teva and American woolwear veteran Pendleton. In-store accessories include Han's own range of painfully cool eyewear. (www.hankjobenhavn.com; Vognmagergade 7, 52 15 35 07; ⊙11am-6pm Mon-Fri, 10am-5pm Sat; ⊠350S, ⓂKongens Nytorv)

Wood Wood
FASHION & ACCESSORIES

27 Map p46, G2

Unisex Wood Wood's flagship store is a solid spot for distinctive street fashion. Top of the heap are Wood Wood's own playful creations, made with superlative fabrics and attention to detail. The supporting cast includes sneakers, unconventional threads from designers like Comme des Garçons Play, Peter Jansen and Gosha Rubchinskiy, as well as accessories spanning fragrances and wallets to quirky eyewear. (⊉35 35 62 64; www.woodwood.dk; Grønnegade 1; ⊙10.30am-6pm Mon-Thu, to 7pm Fri, to 5pm Sat, noon-4pm Sun; ⊠1A, 26, 350S, ⓂKongens Nytorv)

Explore

Nyhavn & the Royal Quarter

The canal of Nyhavn (pronouned 'new-hown') was long a haunt for sailors and writers, including Hans Christian Andersen. These days it lures tourists with its colourful gabled town houses, ship masts and foaming ale. Behind its bustle is blue-blooded Frederiksstaden, home to the royal palace, Marmorkirken (Marble Church) and, further north, the less impressive Little Mermaid.

The Sights in a Day

☀ Fuel up with breakfast at **Union Kitchen** (p67), then head east along **Nyhavn** (p64) to the harbour. Turn left and you'll hit **Skuespilhuset** (p69), the city's contemporary playhouse. Continue north along the waterfront to royal residence Amalienborg Slot. Drop in on the palace museum or continue to the flamboyantly rococo **Marmorkirken** (p64). From here, **Designmuseum Danmark** (p60) is just up Bredgade.

☀ After lunching at the museum, head north to **Kastellet** (p65), home to panoramic ramparts and a gaggle of eccentric historic buildings. If you must drop in on the **Little Mermaid** (p66), you'll find it just to the east of Kastellet, right in the harbour. Close by is artist Bjørn Nørgaard's dystopian modern version.

☾ Unwind with interesting wines at **Den Vandrette** (p68) or **Nebbiolo** (p68) and reserve a table at **Rebel** (p66). Alternatively, dine casually at **Gorm's** (p67) or **District Tonkin** (p66). For a touch of romance, reserve tickets to the ballet or the opera at **Det Kongelige Teater** (p68).

◉ Top Sights

Designmuseum Danmark (p60)

♥ Best of Copenhagen

Museums & Galleries
Designmuseum Danmark (p60)

Kunsthal Charlottenborg (p65)

Drinking
Den Vandrette (p68)

Nebbiolo (p68)

Danish Design
Designmuseum Danmark (p60)

Klassik Moderne Møbelkunst (p69)

Getting There

Ⓜ **Metro** Kongens Nytorv station lies 200m southwest of Nyhavn.

🚌 **Bus** Route 1A reaches the Royal Quarter and Østerbro and route 26 reaches Statens Museum for Kunst. Catch the 350S for Botanisk Have (Botanic Garden) and Nørrebro. Route 66 runs from Nyhavn to Slotsholmen and onward to Tivoli Gardens and Central Station.

⛴ **Boat** Harbour buses stop at Nyhavn.

Top Sights
Designmuseum Denmark

Don't know your Egg from your Swan? What about your PH4 from your PH5? For a crash course in Danish design, head for Designmuseum Danmark. Housed in a converted 18th-century hospital, the museum is a must for fans of the applied arts and industrial design, its collection exploring the evolution of one of the world's most emulated design cultures.

◉ Map p62, C4

www.designmuseum.dk

Bredgade 68

adult/child 100kr/free

🕑 11am-5pm Tue & Thu-Sun, to 9pm Wed

🚌 1A, Ⓜ Kongens Nytorv

Furniture exhibition, Designmuseum Denmark

Twentieth-Century Crafts & Design

This is the museum's hero permanent exhibition, exploring 20th-century industrial design and crafts in the context of social, economic, technological and theoretical changes. You'll find a wealth of Danish design classics, among them Børge Mogensen's Shaker table. One small room dedicated to Arne Jacobsen features objects the architect specifically created for his SAS Royal Hotel. More unusual highlights include Henningsen's steel, timber and leather PH Grand Piano, as well as a wall of vintage graphic posters that includes the work of Viggo Vagnby, creator of the iconic 1959 'Wonderful Copenhagen' poster.

Fashion & Fabric

A notable permanent exhibition is *Fashion & Fabric,* a showcase for the museum's rich cachet of textiles, fashion and accessories. Broken down into three main themes – Design and Decoration, Handicrafts and Industry, and Body and Identity – the 500-plus items on display span four centuries of production. And while the booty includes international creations, the focus is on Danish ingenuity, whether it be brocaded rococo silk dresses and corded-quilted gowns, *hedebo* embroidery or millinery.

Temporary Exhibitions

The museum's rotating temporary exhibitions provide fresh insights into the collection and design in general. Recent shows include *Learning from Japan,* an exploration of the role traditional Japanese crafts and applied arts have played in the development of Danish design. Other temporary offerings have included a pop-up exhibition dedicated to Finnish architect Alvar Aalto and his modernist masterpiece, Paimio Sanatorium.

☑ Top Tip

▶ The museum shop is one of the city's best. You'll find beautiful, design-orientated books, unique ceramics, glassware and jewellery. You'll also find a small selection of Copenhagen-designed fashion pieces.

✗ Take a Break

▶ Head to the museum's **Klint Cafe** (☏ 33 18 56 86; https://designmuseum.dk/besog-os/cafe; smørrebrød 60-85kr; ⊙10am-5.30pm Tue & Thu-Sun, to 8.30pm Wed) for salads, *smørrebrød* and sweet treats. In the warmer months, diners can kick back in the museum's historic, leafy courtyard.

▶ If it's dinnertime, savour seasonal dishes, cured meats and quality wines at nearby Pluto (p94).

CHRISTIANSHAVN

Orlogsværftet

Holmen

Papiroen
(Paper
Island)

Inderhavnen

N

200 m
0.1 miles

Toldbodgade

Amaliehaven

Kvæsthusgraven

15

Sankt Annæ Plads

Kvæsthusgade

Amalienborg
Slotsplad

Slot 2

Frederiksgade

Marmorkirken

Amaliegade

Toldbodgade

Nyhavn 1

Nyhavnsbro

Holbergsgade

13

Havnegade

NYHAVN

Bredgade

11

Lille Strandstr

9

Nyhavn

Nyhavn

Helsingørsgade

Herluf Trolles Gade

Holbergsgade

Store Strandstr

Peder Skrams Gade

7

8

Dronningens Tværgade

6

10

Store Kongensgade

Landgreven

16

Kongens
Nytorv

5

Kunsthal
Charlottenborg

Kongens Nytorv

14

Holmens
Kanal

Tordenskjoldsgade

Niels Juels Gade

Adelgade

Gothersgade

Ny Adelgade

Hovedvagtsgade

Østergade

Lille Kongensgade

Holmens
Kanal

Holmens Kanal

Kronprinsessegade

Ny Østergade

Bremerholm

Højbro
Plads

Fortunstræde

Dybens Gade

Læksgade

Holmens
Bro

Sights

Nyhavn
CANAL

1 ◎ Map p62, C7

There are few nicer places to be on a sunny day than sitting at the outdoor tables of a cafe on the quayside of the Nyhavn canal. The canal was built to connect Kongens Nytorv to the harbour and was long a haunt for sailors and writers, including Hans Christian Andersen. He wrote *The Tinderbox, Little Claus and Big Claus* and *The Princess and the Pea* while living at number 20, and also spent time living at numbers 18 and 67. (Nyhavn; 🚌1A, 26, 66, 350S, M Kongens Nytorv)

Amalienborg Slot
PALACE

2 ◎ Map p62, C5

Home of the current queen, Margrethe II, Amalienborg Slot consists of four austere 18th-century palaces around a large cobbled square. The changing of the guard takes place here daily at noon, the new guard having marched through the city centre from the barracks on Gothersgade at 11.30am.

One of the palaces features exhibits of the royal apartments used by three generations of the monarchy from 1863 to 1947, its reconstructed rooms decorated with gilt-leather tapestries, trompe l'oeil paintings, family photographs and antiques. They include the study and drawing room of Christian IX (1863–1906) and Queen Louise, whose six children wedded into nearly as many royal families – one ascending to the throne in Greece and another marrying Russian Tsar Alexander III. The grand, neoclassical Gala Hall houses statues of Euterpe and Terpsichore created by a young Bertel Thorvaldsen. (📞33 15 32 86; www.kongernessamling.dk/amalienborg; Amalienborg Plads; adult/child 95kr/free; ⌚10am-5pm daily mid-Jun–mid-Sep, reduced hours rest of year; 🚌1A, 26)

Marmorkirken
CHURCH

3 ◎ Map p62, C5

Consecrated in 1894, the neo-baroque Marble Church (officially Frederikskirken) is one of Copenhagen's most imposing architectural assets. Its grandiose dome – inspired by St Peter's in Rome and the largest church dome in Scandinavia – offers an impressive view over the city. The church was ordered by Frederik V and drawn up by Nicolai Eigtved. Construction began in 1749 but spiralling costs saw the project mothballed. Salvation came in the form of Denmark's wealthiest 19th-century financier CF Tietgen, who bankrolled the project's revival. (Marble Church; 📞33 15 01 44; www.marmorkirken.dk; Frederiksgade 4; dome adult/child 35/20kr, church admission free; ⌚church 10am-5pm Mon-Thu & Sat, from noon Fri & Sun, dome 1pm daily mid-Jun–Aug, 1pm Sat & Sun rest of year; 🚌1A)

BIRUTE VIJEIKIENE/SHUTTERSTOCK ©

Guards patrol Amalienborg Slot

Kastellet FORTRESS

4 ◉ Map p62, D1

The star-shaped fortress of Kastellet was originally commissioned by Frederik III in 1662. Today, it is one of the most historically evocative sites in the city, its grassy ramparts and moat surrounding some beautiful 18th-century barracks, as well as a chapel occasionally used for concerts. On the ramparts is a historic windmill, and you get some excellent views of the harbour and Marmorkirken's Vatican-like dome. Just beyond the fortress' southeastern edge is Anders Bundgaard's monumental **Gefion Fountain**, depicting the Norse goddess Gefion. (🚌1A, ⛴Nordre Toldbod)

Kunsthal Charlottenborg MUSEUM

5 ◉ Map p62, B7

Fronting Kongens Nytorv, Charlottenborg was built in 1683 as a palace for the royal family. Home to Det Kongelige Kunstakademi (Royal Academy of Fine Arts) since 1754, it is also a spacious venue for topical contemporary art from homegrown and international names. Expect anything from site-specific installations and video art to painting and sculpture. Admittedly, shows here can be a little hit or miss, so check what's on before heading in. (☎33 74 46 39; www.kunsthalcharlottenborg. dk; Nyhavn 2; adult/child 75kr/free, after 5pm Wed free; ⏱noon-8pm Tue-Fri, 11am-5pm Sat & Sun; 🚌1A, 26, 350S, Ⓜ Kongens Nytorv)

Understand
The Little Mermaid

Love it or loathe it, when the world thinks of Copenhagen, the **Little Mermaid** (Den Lille Havfrue; Langelinie, Østerport; 🚌1A, ⛴Nordre Toldbod) often springs to mind. Alas, many people do seem to loathe this tiny statue of one of Hans Christian Andersen's most famous characters. Commissioned by Carlsberg Brewery and created by sculptor Edvard Eriksen in 1913, the fin-tipped local has been vandalised repeatedly, losing her head and arms more than once. In 2006 Carlsberg commissioned Bjørn Nørgaard (among others) to create a new Little Mermaid. The Danish artist came up with a 'genetically altered' version that sits not far from the original beside the harbour and is, in fact, probably truer in spirit to the rather bleak, twisted Andersen fairy tale.

Eating

Rebel
DANISH $$$

6 🍴 Map p62, B5

Smart, split-level Rebel dishes out arresting, modern Danish grub without the fanfare. The dining space is relatively small, simple and unadorned, giving all the attention to inspired creations like braised octopus with crispy chicken, sage and mushroom foam, or a ravioli of fried wild mushrooms, snail, ginger and soy. Trust the sommelier's wine choices, which include extraordinary Old and New World drops. (☏33 32 32 09; www.restaurantrebel.dk; Store Kongensgade 52; small dishes 115-175kr; ⏱5.30pm-midnight Tue-Sat; 🚌1A, 26, Ⓜ Kongens Nytorv)

District Tonkin
VIETNAMESE $

7 🍴 Map p62, B5

With a playful interior channelling the streets of Vietnam, casual, convivial District Tonkin peddles fresh, gut-filling bánh mì, stuffed with coriander, fresh chilli and combos like Vietnamese sausage with marinated pork, homemade pâté and BBQ sauce. The menu also includes gorgeous, less-common Vietnamese soups, among them tomato-based *xíu mai* (with pork and mushroom meatballs). (☏60 88 86 98; http://district-tonkin.com; Dronningens Tværgade 12; baguettes 54-62kr; ⏱11am-9.30pm Sun-Wed, to 11pm Thu-Sat; 🚌1A, 26, Ⓜ Kongens Nytorv)

AOC
NEW NORDIC $$$

8 🍴 Map p62, B5

In the vaulted cellar of a 17th-century mansion, this intimate, two-starred Michelin standout thrills with evocative, often surprising Nordic flavour combinations, scents and textures. Here, sea scallops might conspire with fermented asparagus, while grilled cherries share the plate with smoked marrow and pigeon breast. Diners choose from two tasting menus, and reservations should be made around a week in advance, especially for late-week dining. (☑33 11 11 45; www.restaurantaoc.dk; Dronningens Tværgade 2; tasting menus 1500-1800kr; ☺6.30pm-12.30am Tue-Sat; 🤶; 🚃1A, 26, Ⓜ Kongens Nytorv)

Gorm's
PIZZA $$

9 🍴 Map p62, C7

Right on Nyhavn canal, rustic, wood-beamed Gorm's is one of the city's best pizza joints. The bases here are thin, crispy and made with sourdough. Toppings are high quality, with both Italian imports and local artisanal items (Funen lamb salami, anyone?). Libations include a handful of local craft beers and a longer cast of cocktails, among them a liquorice-spiked espresso martini. (☑60 40 12 02; www.gormspizza.dk; Nyhavn 14; pizzas 120-145kr; ☺noon-10.30pm Sun-Thu, to 11.30pm Fri & Sat; 🚃66, Ⓜ Kongens Nytorv)

Meyers Bageri
BAKERY $

10 🍴 Map p62, B5

Sugar and spice and all things nice is what you get at this pocket-sized organic bakery, owned by the founding father of the New Nordic food movement, Claus Meyer. Only Danish flour ground in-house is good enough for these sticky morsels, among them golden apple croissants, *blåbærsnurrer* (blueberry twists) and a luscious *kanelsnægel* (cinnamon snail) laced with *remonce* (creamed butter and sugar filling). (www.clausmeyer.dk; Store Kongensgade 46; pastries from 14kr;

☺7am-6pm Mon-Fri, to 4pm Sat & Sun; 🚃1A, 26, Ⓜ Kongens Nytorv)

Union Kitchen
CAFE $$

11 🍴 Map p62, C6

Around the corner from touristy Nyhavn is cognoscenti Union Kitchen, where inked staffers look like punk-pop rockers, the palette is grey on grey, and the clipboard menu is packed with quality, brunch-friendly grub, from yoghurt and granola to burgers and seasonal salads. Top choices include waffles and the 'Balls of the Day', the latter a combo of succulent homemade meatballs served with interesting sides. (Store Strandstræde 21; dishes 79-159kr; ☺7.30am-midnight Mon-Fri, from 8am Sat, 8am-5pm Sun; 🤶; 🚃1A, 66, Ⓜ Kongens Nytorv)

Q Local Life

Forloren Espresso

Coffee snobs weep joyfully into their nuanced espressos and Third-Wave brews at snug, light-filled **Forloren Espresso** (Map p62, B5; www.forlorenespresso.dk; Store Kongensgade 32; ☺8am-4pm Mon-Wed, to 5pm Thu & Fri, 9am-5pm Sat; 🤶; 🚃1A, 26, Ⓜ Kongens Nytorv). Bespectacled owner Niels tends to his brewing paraphernalia like an obsessed scientist, turning UK- and Swedish-roasted beans into smooth, lingering cups of Joe. If you're lucky, you'll score the cosy back nook, the perfect spot to browse Niels' collection of photography tomes.

☑ Top Tip

Mystery Makers

Bring out your inner Detective Sarah Lund with a **Mystery Makers** (📞30 80 30 50; http://mysterymakers. dk; Mystery Hunt per person 250-400kr; ⏱hours vary) interactive mystery hunt. Offered at numerous historical sites around town, players are given fictional identities and a mystery to solve, with a series of riddles and clues along the way. Suitable for adults and kids aged 12 and above, you will need a minimum of four people to form a team. See the website for pricing, which varies according to the day of the week and time of day. (Sunday to Wednesday before 3pm is cheapest.)

Drinking

Nebbiolo   WINE BAR

12 🍷 Map p62, C6

Just off Nyhaven, this smart, contemporary wine bar and shop showcases wines from smaller, inspiring Italian vineyards. Wines by the glass are priced in one of three categories (75/100/125kr) and even those in the lowest price range are often wonderful. (📞60 10 11 09; http://nebbiolo-winebar. com; Store Strandstræde 18; ⏱3pm-midnight Sun-Thu, to 2am Fri & Sat; 📶; 🚌1A, 66, Ⓜ Kongens Nytorv)

Den Vandrette   WINE BAR

13 🍷 Map p62, C8

This is the harbourside wine bar for lauded wine wholesaler **Rosforth & Rosforth** (📞33 32 55 20; www.rosforth. dk; Knippelsbrogade 10; ⏱9am-5pm Mon-Fri, from noon Sat; 🚌2A, 9A, 37, 350S, Ⓜ Christianshavn). The focus is on natural and biodynamic drops, its short, sharply curated list of wines by the glass often including lesser-known blends like Terret Bourret–Vermentino. Guests are welcome to browse the cellar and pick their own bottle. Come summer, it has alfresco waterside tables and deckchairs for sun-kissed toasting. (📞72 14 82 28; www.denvandrette.dk; Havnegade 53A; ⏱4-11pm Tue-Thu & Sun, to midnight Fri, 2pm-midnight Sat; 🚌66, ⛴Nyhaven)

Entertainment

Det Kongelige Teater   BALLET, OPERA

14 ⭐ Map p62, B7

These days, the main focus of the opulent Gamle Scene (Old Stage) is world-class opera and ballet, including productions from the Royal Danish Ballet. The current building, the fourth theatre to occupy the site, was completed in 1872 and designed by Vilhelm Dahlerup and Ove Petersen. Book tickets in advance. (Royal Theatre; 📞33 69 69 69; https://kglteater.dk; Kongens Nytorv; 🚌1A, 26, 350S, Ⓜ Kongens Nytorv)

Skuespilhuset

Skuespilhuset
THEATRE

15 ⭐ Map p62, D7

Copenhagen's harbourside playhouse is home to the Royal Danish Theatre and a world-class repertoire of home-grown and foreign plays. Productions range from the classics to provocative contemporary works. Tickets often sell out well in advance, so book ahead if you're set on a particular production. English-language tours (120kr) are available in July and August; see the website for details. (Royal Danish Playhouse; ☎ 33 69 69 69; https://kglteater.dk; Sankt Anne Plads 36; �🚌66, 🚢Nyhavn, Ⓜ Kongens Nytorv)

Shopping

Klassik Moderne Møbelkunst
DESIGN

16 🅐 Map p62, B6

Close to Kongens Nytorv, Klassik Moderne Møbelkunst is Valhalla for lovers of Danish design, with a trove of classics from greats like Poul Henningsen, Hans J Wegner, Arne Jacobsen, Finn Juhl and Nanna Ditzel – in other words, a veritable museum of Scandinavian furniture from the mid-20th century. (☎ 33 33 90 60; www.klassik.dk; Bredgade 3; �🕐11am-6pm Mon-Fri, 10am-4pm Sat; �🚌1A, 26, 350S, Ⓜ Kongens Nytorv)

Explore

Christianshavn

Christianshavn channels Amsterdam with its snug canals, outdoor cafes and alternative attitude. The quarter was established by Christian IV in the early 17th century as a commercial centre and also as a military buffer for the expanding city. Equally reminiscent of hyper-liberal Amsterdam is the area's most famous attraction, the hash-scented, live-and-let-live commune of Christiania.

The Sights in a Day

☀ Burn off breakfast climbing the landmark spiral tower of **Vor Frelsers Kirke** (p77). Your reward is a breathtaking view of the city. From here, it's a gentle walk to **Christiania** (p72), Copenhagen's ramshackle heart of alternative living. Make sure to explore the ramparts at its eastern end, where the air is bucolic and the architecture eclectic.

☀ Lunch at pretty, herbivorous **Morgenstedet** (p80), then squeeze into Henrik Vibskov's **Den Plettede Gris** (p81) for an arty caffeine fix. Recharged, continue north to ponder architect Henning Larsen's controversial **Operaen** (p81). Alternatively, catch a contemporary art exhibition at **Overgaden** (p77).

☾ Christianshavn is home to three of the city's top restaurants. Assuming you don't have a reservation at **Kadeau** (p78), book a table at **108** (p78) or **Barr** (p80), both respected for their skilful takes on Nordic flavours. If it's Wednesday or later in the week, cap the night with live tunes at still-rocking veteran **Loppen** (p75).

◉ Top Sights

Christiania (p72)

♥ Best of Copenhagen

Eating

Kadeau (p78)

108 (p78)

Entertainment

Operaen (p81)

Loppen (p75)

Getting There

Ⓜ **Metro** Christianshavn station is on Torvegade, Christianshavn's main thoroughfare.

Bus Routes 2A, 40 and 350 cross Christianshavn along Torvegade. Routes 2A and 37 reach Tivoli Gardens and Central Station. Route 350S reaches Nørrebro. Bus 9A reaches Christiania and Operaen.

⛴ **Boat** Harbour buses stop at Operaen. Alternatively, disembark at Nyhavn and cross the Inderhavnsbroen pedestrian bridge to Christianshavn.

Top Sights
Christiania

Picturesque Christiania is more about its canals, historic streets and leafy ramparts than must-see sights. One exception is world-famous commune Christiania, the city's stubbornly idealistic '1970s child'. The commune is within easy walking distance of Christianshavn metro station and its canal-side location makes it a beautiful spot for a quiet waterside saunter. The historic, architecturally unique Vor Freslers Kirke and Christians Kirke are also within easy walking distance of the metro station. North of Christianshavn, the island of Holmen is home to Copenhagen's contemporary, statement-making Operæn.

👁 Map p76, C3

www.christiania.org

Prinsessegade

🚌9A, Ⓜ Christianshavn

Graffiti art, Christiania

Dyssen

Dyssen is Christiania's best-kept secret. This long, pencil-thin rampart on the eastern side of the old city moat is connected to Christiania's eastern edge by bridge. Running north–south along the rampart is a 2km-long path, studded with beautiful maples and ash, hawthorn, elder and wild cherry trees, not to mention the homes of some rather fortunate Christianites. It's a perfect spot for lazy ambling, slow bike rides or some quiet downtime by the water among the swans, herons, moorhens and coots. Some locals even head here to forage for edible snails. Yet Dyssen has a dark past. The rampart was the site of Denmark's last execution ground, where 29 convicted Nazi sympathisers faced the firing squad following the country's postwar trials. The final execution, taking place in 1950, was of Niels Rasmus Ib Birkedal Hansen, the most senior Danish member of the Gestapo. Eerily, the concrete floor and drain are still visible by the path at the northern end of Dyssen.

Stadens Museum for Kunst

Christianites refer to Christiania as 'Staden' (The Town), and the name of art gallery Stadens Museum for Kunst is a tongue-in-cheek play on the more 'establishment' Statens Museum for Kunst. You'll find the place on the 2nd floor of the Loppen building, a former artillery warehouse dating from 1863 and flanking Prinsessegade, just beside Christiania's main entrance. Head up for rotating exhibitions of contemporary art, spanning both local and international artists, and covering anything from drawings and paintings to installations. In any given month you might be poring over Greenlandic stoneware, recycled Tunisian sculpture or local photography. The gallery also houses a petite

☑ Top Tips

▶ From late June to the end of August, 60- to 90-minute guided tours (40kr) of Christiania run daily at 3pm (weekends only September to late June). Tours commence just inside Christiania's main entrance on Prinsessegade.

▶ While taking photos in Christiania is generally fine, don't snap pictures on or around the main drag of Pusher St. The area is lined with illegal cannabis dealers who can become nervous or aggressive if photographed.

✗ Take a Break

For affordable vegetarian grub in a pretty garden, make a beeline for Morgenstedet (p80), located in the heart of Christiania.

For a more upmarket dinner, reserve a table at Michelin-starred, modern-Danish hotspot 108 (p78), located 650m north of Christiania.

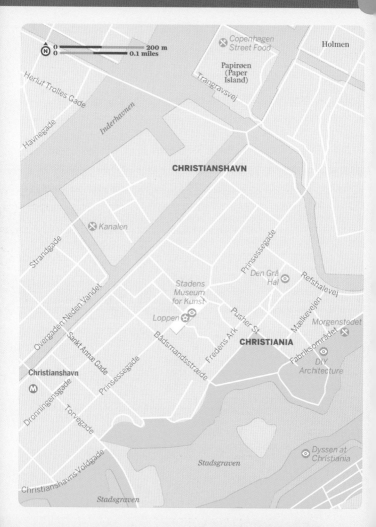

cafe for any caffeine-fuelled art debate you may be itching to have.

Den Grå Hal

The Grey Hall is the commune's largest cultural venue, able to pack in around 1500 people. It was built in 1893, originally as a riding hall for the military. With the establishment of Freetown Christiania, the space found new purpose as a hub for art and music. Some of the biggest names in music have rocked its weathered walls over the years, among them Bob Dylan, Metallica and Manic Street Preachers. While its calendar is hardly jam-packed these days, the building is worth a look for its architecture and colourful graffiti. In December Den Grå Hal becomes the focal point for Christiania's Christmas festivities.

DIY Architecture

Beyond its graffiti-strewn barrack buildings, Christiania is home to some of the city's most eclectic, imaginative architecture. Much of this is in the form of 'tiny houses', small abodes built by hand using salvaged materials. Follow the commune's quieter paths and you'll stumble upon a whimsical collection of buildings, from a home made entirely of random window frames to converted greenhouses, German *bauwagens* (wooden caravans) and Roma wagons, and houses on boats and floating platforms. Many of the most intriguing creations are located beside, or close to, the old city moat on Christiania's eastern side.

CAROLINE BOOGAARD/GETTY IMAGES ©

Decorated door, Freetown Christiania

Loppen

Its motto might be 'Going out of business since 1973', but 40-something Loppen (☏ 32 57 84 22; www.loppen.dk; Sydområdet 4B; ☻ 8.30pm-late Sun-Thu, 9pm-late Fri & Sat; ☜) just keeps on rocking. In the same wooden-beamed warehouse as art gallery Stadens Museum for Kunst, the joint started off by spotlighting the local underground scene before evolving into a more prolific music hub. These days, its program serves up an eclectic mix of both local and international talent, from emerging acts to more established names.

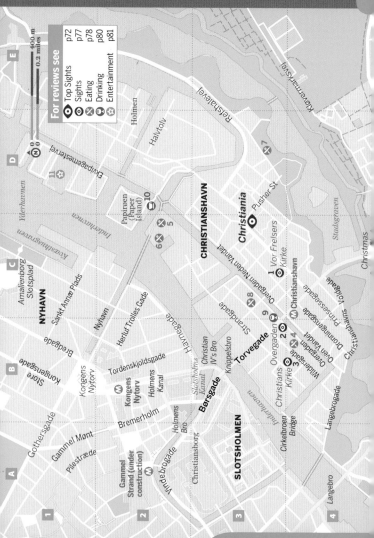

For reviews see

◉	Top Sights	p72
⦿	Sights	p77
✕	Eating	p78
🍷	Drinking	p80
🎭	Entertainment	p81

400 m
0.2 miles

NYHAVN

Amalienborg
Slotsplad

Yderhavnen

Kvæsthusgraven

Inderhavnen

Sankt Annæ Plads

Kongens
Nytorv

Store Kongensgade

Bredgade

Gothersgade

Gammel Mønt

Pilestræde

Herluf Trolles Gade

Nyhavn

Havnegade

Tordenskjoldsgade

Holmens Kanal

Bremerholm

Holmens Bro

Christiansborg

Gammel Strand (under construction)

Vindebrogade

Slotsholmen

Slotsholms Kanal

Børsgade

Christian IV's Bro

Knippelsbro

Torvegade

Christians Kirke

Overgaden Oven Vandet

Wildersgade

Dronningensgade

Prinsessegade

Christianshavns Voldgade

Christianshavn

Overgaden Neden Vandet

Strandgade

Vor Frelsers Kirke

Christiania

Pusher St

Refshalevej

Halvtolv

Holmen

Papirøen (Paper Island)

Ekvipagemestervej

Cirkelbroen Bridge

Langebrogade

Langebro

Christmas

Stadsgraven

View from Vor Frelsers Kirke

Sights

Vor Frelsers Kirke

CHURCH

1 Map p76, C3

It's hard to miss this 17th-century church and its 95m-high spiral tower. For a soul-stirring city view, make the head-spinning 400-step ascent to the top – the last 150 steps run along the outside rim of the tower, narrowing to the point where they literally disappear at the top. Inspired by Borromini's tower of St Ivo in Rome, the spire was added in 1752 by Lauritz de Thurah. Inside the church, highlights include an ornate baroque altar and elaborately carved pipe organ from 1698. (41 66 63 57; www.vorfrelserskirke.dk; Sankt Annæ Gade 29; church free, tower adult/child 40/10kr; 11am-3.30pm, closed during services, tower 9.30am-7pm Mon-Sat, 10.30am-7pm Sun May-Sep, reduced hours rest of year; 2A, 9A, 37, 350S, Christianshavn)

Overgaden

GALLERY

2 Map p76, B3

Rarely visited by tourists, this non-profit art gallery runs about 10 exhibitions annually, putting the spotlight on contemporary installation art and photography, usually by younger artists, both Danish and international. The gallery also runs a busy calendar of artist talks, lectures, performances, concerts and film screenings. See the website for upcoming events.

(📞32 57 72 73; www.overgaden.org; Over-gaden Neden Vandet 17; admission free; 🕐1-5pm Tue, Wed & Fri-Sun, to 8pm Thu; 🚌2A, 9A, 37, 350S, Ⓜ Christianshavn)

Christians Kirke
CHURCH

3 ◉ Map p76, B4

Named in honour of Christian IV – who founded Christianshavn in the early 17th century – Christians Kirke is well known for its unusual rococo interior. This includes tiered viewing galleries more reminiscent of a theatre than a place of worship. The church was built between 1754 and 1759, serving Christianshavn's sizeable German congregation until the end of the 19th century. (📞32 54 15 76; www.christians kirke.dk; Strandgade 1; 🕐10am-4pm Tue-Fri; 🚌2A, 9A, 37, 350S, Ⓜ Christianshavn)

☑️ Top Tip

GoBoat

The **GoBoat** (Map p76, A1; 📞40 26 10 25; www.goboat.dk; Islands Brygge 10; boat hire 1/2/3hr 399/749/999kr; 🕐9.30am-sunset; 👶; 🚌5C, 12, Ⓜ Islands Brygge) kiosk beside Islands Brygge Havnebadet rents out small solar-powered boats that let you explore Copenhagen's harbour and canals independently. You don't need prior sailing experience and each comes with a built-in picnic table (you can buy supplies at GoBoat or bring your own). Boats seat up to eight and rates are per boat, so the more in your group, the cheaper per person.

Eating

Kadeau
NEW NORDIC $$$

4 🍴 Map p76, B4

The big-city spin-off of the Bornholm original, this Michelin-two-starred standout has firmly established itself as one of Scandinavia's top New Nordic restaurants. Whether it's salted and burnt scallops drizzled with clam bouillon, or an unexpected combination of toffee, crème fraiche, potatoes, radish and elderflower, each dish evokes Nordic flavours, moods and landscapes with extraordinary creativity and skill.

The wine list is a thrilling, enlightening showcase of smaller producers and natural drops, and service is warm, genuine and knowledgeable. Book ahead. (📞33 25 22 23; www.kadeau. dk; Wildersgade 10B; tasting menu 1800kr; 🕐6.30pm-midnight Wed-Fri, noon-4pm & 6.30pm-midnight Sat; 🚌2A, 9A, 37, 350S, Ⓜ Christianshavn)

108
DANISH $$

5 🍴 Map p76, C2

In a soaring, concrete-pillared warehouse, 108 offers a more casual, accessible take on New Nordic cuisine than its world-renowned sibling Noma. The family-style sharing-plate menu is all about seasonal, locally sourced ingredients, farmed or foraged, preserved, fermented and pickled. While not all dishes hit the mark, many leave a lasting impression. Three dishes per diner should satiate most appetites. (📞32 96 32 92; www.108.dk; Strandgade 108; dishes

Understand

The Danish Table

Not only is Copenhagen home to 15 Michelin stars, it's also the stomping ground of an ever-expanding league of bold, brilliant young chefs turning top produce into groundbreaking innovations and putting new verve into long-loved classics. So grab a (beautifully designed) fork and find a spot at the coveted Danish table.

Beyond New Nordic

While the New Nordic cuisine served at hotspot restaurants like Michelin-starred Kadeau continues to thrill food critics, bloggers and general gluttons, Copenhagen's food scene continues to evolve. Numerous chefs from high-end kitchens have since opened their own restaurants, among them 108, Restaurant Mes and Bror. Most of these offer simpler, more affordable food but don't skimp on quality and innovation: a 'democratisation' of the gourmet dining experience. Many are also taking a less dogmatic approach to contemporary Nordic cooking, using the odd non-regional influence or spice without fear of Nordic culinary damnation. A Noma alumnus is behind hugely popular taquería Hija de Sanchez, one of a growing number of casual, high-quality international eateries that also includes Slurp Ramen Joint.

Danish Classics

Despite the New Nordic revolution, old-school Danish fare remains a major player on the city's tables. Indeed, tucking into classics such as *frikadeller* (meatballs), *sild* (pickled herring) and Denmark's most famous culinary export, *smørrebrød*(open sandwiches), at institutions such as Schønnemann is an integral part of the Copenhagen experience. The basic smørrebrød is a slice of bread topped with any number of ingredients, from roast beef or pork to juicy shrimps, pickled herring, liver pâté or fried fish fillet. The garnishes are equally variable,with the sculptured final product often looking too good to eat. In the laws of Danish smørrebrød, smoked salmon is served on white bread, and herring on rye bread. Whatever the combination, the iconic dish is best paired with akvavit and an invigorating beer.

95-185kr, sharing dishes for 2 people 300-450kr; ⏱restaurant 5pm-midnight, cafe 8am-midnight Mon-Fri, from 9am Sat & Sun; 🛜; 🚌9A)

Barr

SCANDINAVIAN $$$

6 🍴 Map p76, C2

Meaning 'barley' in old Norse, oak-lined Barr offers polished, produce-driven takes on old North Sea traditions. The small plates are a little hit and miss, with standouts including sourdough pancakes with caviar. You'll need about four small plates per person; a better-value option is to savour the pancakes and fill up on the fantastic schnitzel or *frikadeller* (Danish meatballs). (☑32 96 32 93; http://restaurantbarr.com; Strandgade 93; small dishes 75-240kr, 4-course menu 600kr; ⏱5pm-midnight Tue-Thu, from noon Sat & Sat; 🛜; 🚌9A, 66, ⛴Nyhavn)

Morgenstedet

VEGETARIAN $

7 🍴 Map p76, D3

A homey, hippy bolthole in the heart of Christiania, Morgenstedet offers a short, simple blackboard menu. There's usually one soup, plus two or three mains with a choice of side salads. Whether it's cauliflower soup with chickpeas and herbs or creamy potato gratin, options are always vegetarian, organic and delicious, not to mention best devoured in the blissful cafe garden. Cash only. (Fabriksområdet 134; dishes 50-110kr; ⏱noon-9pm Tue-Sun; 🛜🍴; 🚌9A, ⓂChristianshavn)

Cafe Wilder

DANISH $$

8 🍴 Map p76, C3

With its crisp white linen and circular sidewalk tables, this corner classic feels like a Parisian neighbourhood bistro. It's actually one of Copenhagen's oldest cafes, featured several times in the cult TV series *Borgen*. Relive your favourite scenes over beautiful lunchtime smørrebrød (open sandwiches) or Franco-Danish dinner mains like tender Danish pork with sweet-potato croquette and a blackcurrant sauce. (☑32 54 71 83; www.cafewilder. dk; Wildersgade 56; lunch 119-149kr, dinner mains 179-209kr; ⏱9am-11pm Mon-Thu, to midnight Fri & Sat, to 10.30pm Sun; 🛜; 🚌2A, 9A, 37, 350S, ⓂChristianshavn)

Drinking

Christianshavns Bådudlejning og Café

BAR

9 🍺 Map p76, C3

Right on Christianshavn's main canal, this festive, wood-decked cafe-bar is a wonderful spot for drinks by the water. It's a cosy, affable hang-out, with jovial crowds and strung lights. There's grub for the peckish and gas heaters and tarpaulins to ward off any northern chill. The cafe plans to resume its rental of little rowboats in 2018. (☑32 96 53 53; www.baadudlejningen. dk; Overgaden Neden Vandet 29; ⏱9am-midnight Jun-Aug, reduced hours rest of year; 🛜; 🚌2A, 9A, 37, 350S, ⓂChristianshavn)

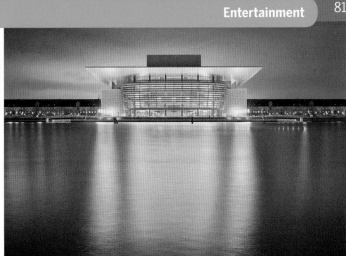

MITJA SCHNEEHAGE/500PX ©

Operæn (Copenhagen Opera House)

Den Plettede Gris CAFE

10 🚇 Map p76, D2

The pocket-sized 'Spotted Pig' on Papirøen (Paper Island) belongs to Danish designer, artist, musician and all-round avant-gardiste Henrik Vibskov. Inside, the space is pure Vibskov, with elastic-band wall sculptures, splashes of pink and red, and an effortlessly cool, chilled-out vibe. Stop by for Swedish-roasted coffee or organic tea and cake, or guzzle boutique beers with ingredients like elderflower. (Trangravsvej 5; ⊘9am-6pm Mon-Fri, from 10am Sat & Sun; 🛜; 🚌9A, 🚢Papirøen)

Entertainment

Operæn OPERA

11 ⭐ Map p76, D1

Designed by the late Henning Larsen, Copenhagen's state-of-the-art opera house has two stages: the Main Stage and the smaller, more experimental Takkeløftet. The repertoire runs the gamut from blockbuster classics to contemporary opera. While the occasional opera is sung in English, all subtitles are in Danish only. Tickets can be booked directly via the website. (Copenhagen Opera House; ☑box office 33 69 69 69; www.kglteater.dk; Ekvipagemestervej 10; 🚌9A, 🚢Operaen)

Nørreport

Nørreport and its surrounds blend market stalls, restaurants and bars with distinguished art collections. You'll find appetite-piquing Torvehallerne KBH and the quietly hip strip of Nansensgade, dotted with atmospheric eating and drinking spots. The area is also home to several flagship sights, among them Denmark's National Gallery and Rosenborg Slot. The latter skirts manicured Kongens Have.

The Sights in a Day

☀ Breakfast at **Torvehallerne KBH** (p90), where gourmet oats await at made-from-scratch **Grød** (p90). While this particular stall opens early, most of the market vendors open at 10am (11am on Sunday), so time your visit for a postbreakfast market saunter. Cross tranquil **Botanisk Have** (p93) on your way to **Statens Museum for Kunst** (p88), where many of the country's greatest masterpieces await.

☀ Close by, elegant Kongens Have is home to **Orangeriet** (p85), which serves gorgeous smørrebrød (open sandwiches) at lunch. Mouth wiped, cross the park to Renaissance-era **Rosenborg Slot** (p84), home to the crown jewels. Dazzling assets are also in abundance at nearby **Davids Samling** (p93), known for its superlative hoard of Islamic decorative arts.

☾ Come evening, opt for low-key cool on Nansensgade. Oenophiles will swoon at the choice of wines at **Bibendum** (p95), while fans of kooky interiors will appreciate offbeat **Bankeråt** (p95). For a thrilling, affordable New Nordic dinner, book a table at **Höst** (p94). Otherwise tuck into honest, flavour-packed dishes at **Pluto** (p94).

For a local's day in Nørreport, see p90.

◉ Top Sights

Rosenborg Slot (p84)

Statens Museum for Kunst (p88)

○ Local Life

To Market, To Market

♥ Best of Copenhagen

Museums & Galleries

Rosenborg Slot (p84)

Statens Museum for Kunst (p88)

Davids Samling (p93)

Eating

Höst (p94)

Pluto (p94)

Getting There

Ⓜ **Metro** Nørreport station is right beside Torvehallerne KBH.

🚆 **S-Train** All S-train lines stop at Nørreport station. Catch a Helsingør-bound regional train to Humlebæk for Louisiana art museum.

🚌 **Bus** Routes 5C and 350S reach Nørrebro. Bus 14 runs through central Copenhagen and is handy for Slotsholmen. Route 6A reaches Vesterbo and Frederiksberg.

Top Sights
Rosenborg Slot

Moated Rosenborg Slot heaves with blue-blooded portraits and tapestries, royal hand-me-downs and the nation's crown jewels. Built between 1606 and 1633 by Christian IV to serve as his summer home, the Danish royals opened the castle as a museum in the 1830s, while still using it as as their own giant jewellery box. It serves both functions to this day.

👁 Map p92, D3

www.kongernessamling.dk/en/rosenborg

adult/child 110kr/free, incl Amalienborg Slot 145kr/free

🕑9am-5pm mid-Jun–mid-Sep, reduced hours rest of year

🚌6A, 42, 184, 185, 350S, Ⓜ Nørreport, Ⓢ Nørreport

View of Rosenborg Slot from Kongens Have (p87)

Christian IV's Winter Room

Room 1 is the original building's best-preserved room. The rich wooden panelling – adorned with inlaid Dutch paintings – was begun by Court cabinetmaker Gregor Greuss and completed in 1620. Adorning the ceiling are mythological paintings by Danish-born Dutch painter Pieter Isaacsz, the works replacing the room's original stucco ceiling c 1770. Among the room's items is a 17th-century Florentine tabletop, made of inlaid semiprecious stones. Equally fascinating is the Astronomical Clock, which comes with moving figures and musical works. Dating back to 1594, the timepiece was made by the renowned Swiss clockmaker Isaac Habrecht.

Christian IV's Bedroom

It's in room 3 that Denmark's famous 'Builder King', Christian IV, died on 28 February 1648, and it's here that you'll find his nightcap and slippers, as well as the bloodstained clothes from his naval battle of Kolberger Heide in July 1644. The walls, doors and stucco ceiling all date back to Christian IV's time, as does the stucco ceiling in the adjoining toilet. The toilet's fetching blue and white wall tiles date to Frederik IV's refurbishment of the castle in 1705. Some of the tiles are the Dutch original, while others were made in Copenhagen in 1736. Back in the day, a water cistern was used for flushing, with the king's business expelled straight into the moat.

Mirror Cabinet

It mightn't be the 1st floor's most lavish room, but the Mirror Cabinet is certainly its most curious. Inspired by France's Palace of Versailles, the room's mirrored ceiling, floor and walls could sit comfortably on the pages of a 1970s interior design magazine. In reality, the interior is pure

☑ Top Tips

▶ To avoid the queues – which can be dishearteningly long in the peak summer months – buy your ticket online. The ticket can be sent directly to your smartphone so there's no need to print a copy. Also, buying your ticket online ensures you entry in your desired time slot. If you have a Copenhagen Card, however, you will need to obtain your tickets in person at the castle ticket office.

✗ Take a Break

▶ On the other side of Kongens Have, **Big Apple** (http://big-apple.dk; Kronprinsessegade 2; sandwiches 60kr; ⏰8am-6pm Mon-Fri, 9am-6pm Sat & Sun; 🛜; 🚌350S, Ⓜ Kongens Nytorv) is a good spot to grab a freshly made sandwich and coffee.

▶ For something more upscale, book a table at Orangeriet (☎33 11 13 07; www.restaurant-orangeriet.dk; smørrebrod 75kr, 3-/4-/5-course dinner 395/475/525kr; ⏰11.30am-3pm & 6-10pm Mon-Sat, noon-4pm Sun), in the park's former observatory.

baroque, dating back to the beginning of the 18th century and specially designed for Frederik IV. All the rage at the time, mirror cabinets were commonly featured in the innermost sanctum of a king's suite, usually in connection with the royal bedchamber. Frederik IV's bedchamber was downstairs in room 4, connected to the Mirror Cabinet by a spiral staircase. If the thought of all these mirrors seems a little kinky, bear in mind that the adjoining room is where the king kept his collection of erotica.

Knights' Hall

Originally a ballroom, the Knights' Hall was completed in 1624 and was the last of the castle's rooms to be furnished. Gracing the walls are the Rosenborg Tapestries, 12 woven works depicting the battles between Denmark and Sweden during the Scanian War (1675–79). The tapestries were a PR exercise of sorts, commissioned by Christian V to flaunt his military prowess. The Knights' Hall is also home to the coronation thrones and a stucco ceiling with four paintings by Hendrick Krock that represent the four regalia: crown, orb, sword and sceptre. Two small chambers run off the hall, one displaying Venetian glassware, the other home to Royal Copenhagen Porcelain's original Flora Danica set, decorated with exquisite botanical motifs.

Basement Cellar Rooms & Green Room

Rosenborg Slot's undisputed pièce de résistance is its basement, home to an extraordinary collection of royal regalia and gifts. Some of the dusty bottles in the castle cellar date back to the 18th century. The wine is still used on special royal occasions, though it's now merely splashed into more palatable drops as a ceremonial gesture. The northernmost cellar room contains some rather unusual decorative objects, including an 18th-century chandelier made of amber by Lorenz Spengler. At the southern end of the basement is the Green Room, itself laden with intriguing royal paraphernalia. Keep an eye out for Christian IV's riding trappings, used at his coronation in 1596.

Treasury

Just off the Green Room, the Treasury is where you'll find the castle's most valuable treasures. These include Christian IV's spectacular crown, created especially for his coronation by Dirich Fyring in Odense. Made of gold, pearls and table-cut stones and weighing 2.89kg, its features include the figure of a self-pecking pelican feeding its offspring blood (a symbolic representation of the need for rulers to willingly sacrifice their own blood for their subjects.) Other showstoppers include the jewel-studded sword

Reception room, Rosenborg Slot

of Christian III (crafted in 1551) and the obsessively detailed Oldenburg Horn. Made of silver in the mid-15th century, the horn is believed to have been a gift from Christian I to Cologne's cathedral. It found itself in Danish hands once more after the Reformation.

Kongens Have

Fronting Rosenborg Slot is much-loved Kongens Have (King's Garden). The city's oldest park, it was laid out in the early 17th century by Christian IV, who used it as his vegetable patch. These days it has a little more to offer, including wonderfully romantic paths, a fragrant rose garden and some of the longest mixed borders in northern Europe. It's also home to a marionette theatre, with free performances from mid-July to mid-August (2pm and 3pm Tuesday to Sunday). Located on the northeastern side of the park, the theatre occupies one of the neoclassical pavilions designed by 18th-century Danish architect Peter Meyn.

Top Sights
Statens Museum for Kunst

Denmark's National Gallery is the country's pre-eminent art institution, its cachet of paintings, sculpture and immersive works spanning centuries of creative expression, from Mategna to Matisse and beyond. Top billing goes to its homegrown heavyweights: Golden Age icons, such as Christoffer Wilhelm Eckersberg and Christen Købke, 20th-century mavericks Asger Jorn and Per Kirkeby, and current innovators like Elmgreen & Dragset.

👁 Map p92, D1

www.smk.dk

adult/child 110kr/free

🕐 11am-5pm Tue & Thu-Sun, to 8pm Wed

🚌 6A, 26, 42, 184, 185

European Art: 1300–1800
Originally a royal collection, this is where you'll find the museum's Old Masters. These include Rubens' blockbuster *Judgement of Solomon* (c1617). Look out for a series of paintings by 17th-century Flemish artist Cornelis Norbertus Gijsbrechts: trompe l'œils with an astoundingly modern sensibility. Standout Italian works include Andrea Mategna's *Christ as the Suffering Redeemer* (c1495–1500).

Danish & Nordic Art: 1750–1900
Don't miss the quiet rage of Nicolai Abildgaard's *Wounded Philoctetes* (1775) and Johan Christian Dahl's *Winter Landscape near Vordingborg, Denmark* (1829). CW Eckersberg's most celebrated work is *A View through Three Arches of the Third Storey of the Colosseum* (1815–16). What appears to be a faithful panorama of Rome is actually pieced together from three different perspectives.

French Art: 1900–30
SMK's French collection includes an impressive number of works by Henri Matisse. The most famous of these is *Portrait of Madame Matisse* (1905). Also known as *The Green Line,* it's widely considered a masterpiece of modern portrait painting. Other standouts here include André Derain's *Woman in a Chemise* (1906) – a highlight from the artist's Fauvist period.

Modern Danish & International Art
The collection's modern Danish works are especially notable, among them expressionist Jens Søndergaard's brooding *Stormy Sea* (1954) and CoBrA artists such as Asger Jorn. Look out for Bjørn Nørgaard's *The Horse Sacrifice* and *Objects from the Horse Sacrifice,* which document the artist's ritualistic sacrifice of a horse in 1970 to protest the Vietnam War.

☑ Top Tips

▸ Consider exploring the collections with SMK's fantastic audio guide. Selected highlights for the permanent collections are discussed in short, easily digestible interviews with a museum curator.

▸ The museum hosts numerous special events throughout the year. These include SMK Fridays. Held around seven times annually (in spring and autumn), it sees the museum open until late with art talks, DJs, performances and food. Check the website for details.

✕ Take a Break

▸ Just 450m east of the National Gallery, **Aamanns Takeaway** (✆ 20 80 52 01; www.aamanns.dk; Øster Farimagsgade 10; smørrebrød 65-115kr; ⏰ 11am-5.30pm daily, take away 11am-7pm Mon-Fri, to 4pm Sat & Sun; 🚌 6A, 14, 37, 42, 150S, 184, 185) serves some of the best smørrebrød in the city.

Local Life
To Market, To Market

A mouthwatering ode to the fresh, the tasty and the slow, food market **Torvehallerne KBH** (www.torvehallerne kbh.dk; ⏰10am-7pm Mon-Thu, to 8pm Fri, to 6pm Sat, 11am-5pm Sun) peddles everything from seasonal herbs and berries, to smoked meats, seafood and cheeses, smørrebrød, fresh pasta, and hand-brewed coffee. You could easily spend an hour or more exploring its twin glass halls, chatting to the vendors, stocking the larder, and noshing on freshly cooked, sit-down meals.

❶ Grød
Holistic **Grød** (Hall 2, stal A8; http://groed.com) turns stodge sexy with its modern take on porridge. Made-from-scratch options might include porridge with gooseberry compote, liquorice sugar, *skyr* (Icelandic yogurt) and hazelnuts, or healthier-than-thou grain porridge cooked in carrot juice and served with apple, roasted flaxseeds, raisins and a zingy ginger syrup. If it's later in the day, try the chicken congee.

❷ Coffee Collective
Save your caffeine fix for **Coffee Collective** (Hall 2, stall C1; www.coffeecollective.dk). The beans here are sourced ethically and directly from farmers and the team usually offers two espresso

blends: one full-bodied and traditional, the other more stringent and Third Wave in flavour. If espresso is just too passé, order a hand-brewed cup from the Kalita Wave dripper.

❸ Omegn
Nordic deli **Omegn** (Hall 1, stall E2; http://omegn.com) stocks the top products from various small-scale Danish farms and food artisans. The cheese selection includes Thybo, a sharp cow's milk cheese from northern Jutland. Another good buy are the handcrafted Borghgedal beers from Vejle. Peckish punters can nibble on the cheese and charcuterie platter, or go old-school with a warming serve of *skipperlabskov* (beef stew).

❹ Unika
Arla is one of Denmark's mega dairy companies, and **Unika by Arla** (Hall 1, stall F5; www.arlaunika.dk) is its boutique offshoot. The company works with small dairies, artisan cheesemakers and top chefs to produce Nordic-inspired cheeses. Look out for the unpasteurised Kry, which delivers a flavour considered superior to pasteurised cheeses. Equally unique are the apple-based dessert wines from Jutland's Cold Hand Winery.

TORVEHALLERNE

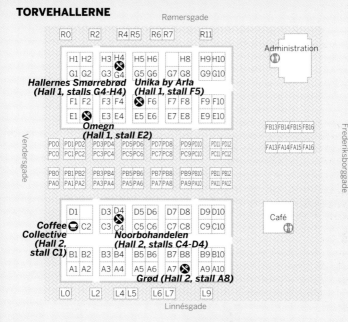

Rømersgade

Administration

Frederiksborgade

Vendersgade

Hallernes Smørrebrød
(Hall 1, stalls G4-H4)

Unika by Arla
(Hall 1, stall F5)

Omegn
(Hall 1, stall E2)

Coffee
Collective
(Hall 2,
stall C1)

Noorbohandelen
(Hall 2, stalls C4-D4)

Grød (Hall 2, stall A8)

Café

Linnésgade

5 Hallernes Smørrebrød

Not only is the smørrebrød scrumptious at **Hallernes Smørrebrød** (Hall 1, stalls G4-H4; www.hallernes.dk), it – like the beers and snaps on offer – is well priced. Grab a spot at the wooden bar, order a Mikkeller beer, and tuck into beautifully presented classics like *fiskefilet* (fish fillet) with remoulade. Order one smørrebrød if you're peckish, two if you're hungry.

6 Noorbohandelen

It's never too early for a skål at **Noorbohandelen** (Hall 2, stall C4-D4; https://www.noorbohandelen.dk) its shelves stocked with limited-edition and small-batch craft spirits to sample and purchase. Options include their own brand of snaps and bitters, infused with herbs from the Danish island of Møn. Best of all, the beautiful, customised bottles will remind you of your Scandi sojourn long after the last pour.

For reviews see

◎ Top Sights	p84
◎ Sights	p93
✕ Eating	p94
◐ Drinking	p95
ⓐ Shopping	p95

KIEV.VICTOR/SHUTTERSTOCK ©

Botanisk Have

Sights

Davids Samling   MUSEUM

1 ◉ Map p92, E3

Davids Samling is a wonderful curiosity of a gallery housing Scandinavia's largest collections of Islamic art, including jewellery, ceramics and silk, and exquisite works such as an Egyptian rock crystal jug from AD 1000 and a 500-year-old Indian dagger inlaid with rubies. And it doesn't end there, with an elegant selection of Danish, Dutch, English and French art, porcelain, silverware and furniture from the 17th to 19th centuries. (☏33 73 49 49; www.davidmus.dk; Kronprinsessegade 30; admission free;

☉10am-5pm Tue & Thu-Sun, to 9pm Wed; 🚌26, 350S, Ⓜ Kongens Nytorv)

Botanisk Have   GARDENS

2 ◉ Map p92, C2

Restorative and romantic, Copenhagen's Botanic Garden lays claim to around 13,000 species of plant life – the largest collection in Denmark. You can amble along tranquil trails, escape to warmer climes in the 19th-century **Palmehus** (☉10am-5pm daily Apr-Sep, 10am-3pm Tue-Sun Oct-Apr; 🚌6A, 14, 37, 150S, 184, 185, Ⓜ Nørreport, Ⓢ Nørreport) glasshouse and even pick up honey made using the garden's own bees at the gorgeous little gift shop. (Botanic Garden; http://botanik.snm.ku.dk; Gothersgade 140, Nørreport; ☉8.30am-6pm Apr-Sep, to 4pm

Tue-Sun Oct-Mar; 🚼; 🚌6A, 42, 150S, 184, 185, Ⓜ Nørreport, Ⓢ Nørreport)

Hirschsprung   MUSEUM

3 ◉ Map p92, D1

Dedicated to Danish art of the 19th and early 20th centuries, Hirschsprungske is a little jewel-box of a gallery, full of wonderful surprises for art lovers unfamiliar with the classic era of Danish oil painting. Originally the private holdings of tobacco magnate Heinrich Hirschsprung, it contains works by 'Golden Age' painters such as Christen Købke and CW Eckersberg, a notable selection by Skagen painters PS Krøyer and Anna and Michael Ancher, and also works by the Danish symbolists and the Funen painters. (☏35 42 03 36; www.hirschsprung.dk; Stockholmsgade 20; adult/child 75kr/free; ⊙11am-4pm Wed-Sun; 🚌6A, 14, 37, 42, 150S)

Eating

Höst   NEW NORDIC $$$

4 🍴 Map p92, A4

Höst's phenomenal popularity is easy to understand: award-winning interiors and New Nordic food that's equally fabulous and filling. The set menu is superb, with three smaller 'surprise dishes' thrown in and evocative creations like baked flounder with roasted chicken skin, shrimp, peas and an apple-vinegar fish stock, or a joyful rose-hip sorbet paired with Danish strawberries, a

green strawberry puree, meringue and herbs. (☏89 93 84 09; www.hostvakst.dk; Nørre Farimagsgade 41; 3-/5-course menu 350/450kr; ⊙5.30pm-midnight, last order 9.30pm; 🚌37, Ⓜ Nørreport, Ⓢ Nørreport)

Pluto   DANISH $$

5 🍴 Map p92, E4

Loud, convivial Pluto is not short of friends, and for good reason: superfun soundtrack, attentive staff and beautiful, simple dishes by respected local chef Rasmus Oubæk. Whether it's flawlessly seared cod with seasonal carrots or a side of new potatoes, funky truffles and green beans in a mussel broth, the family-style menu is all about letting the produce sing. (☏33 16 00 16; http://restaurantpluto.dk/forside; Borgergade 16; mains 135-225kr; ⊙5.30pm-midnight Mon-Thu, to 2am Fri & Sat, to 11pm Sun; 🛜; 🚌1A, 26, Ⓜ Kongens Nytorv)

Atelier September   CAFE $

6 🍴 Map p92, E4

It might look like a *Vogue* photo shoot with its white-on-white interior and vintage glass ceiling (typical of old Danish pharmacies), but Atelier September is very much a cafe. Kitted out in vintage exhibition posters and communal tables, it sells gorgeous espresso and simple, inspired edibles. Standouts include sliced avocado on rye bread, topped with lemon zest, chives, paprika and peppery olive oil. (☏26 29 57 53; www.atelierseptember.dk; Gothersgade 30; dishes 30-125kr; ⊙7.30am-4pm Mon-Fri, from 9am Sat, from 10am Sun; 🚌350S, Ⓜ Kongens Nytorv)

Drinking

Bibendum   WINE BAR

7 🚇 Map p92, A3

In a snug cellar on Nansensgade, Bibendum is an oenophile's best friend. While the savvy wine list offers over 30 wines by the glass, always ask the barkeeps what's off the menu. On our last visit, this included a spectacular Pinot Noir from the Czech Republic. The vibe is intimate but relaxed and the menu of small plates (80kr to 95kr) simply gorgeous. (☏33 33 07 74; http://bibendum.dk; Nansensgade 45; ⏱4pm-midnight Mon-Sat; 🛜; 🚌37, 5C, 350S, 🅼Nørreport, 🆂Nørreport)

Culture Box   CLUB

8 🚇 Map p92, E2

Electronica connoisseurs swarm to Culture Box, known for its impressive local and international DJ line-ups and sharp sessions of electro, techno, house and drum'n'bass. The club is divided into three spaces: preclubbing Culture Box Bar, intimate club space Red Box, and heavyweight Black Box, where big-name DJs play the massive sound system. (☏33 32 50 50; www.culture-box.com; Kronprinsessegade 54A; ⏱Culture Box Bar 6pm-1am Thu-Sat, Red Box 11pm-late Fri & Sat, Black Box midnight-late Fri & Sat; 🚌26)

Bankeråt   BAR

9 🚇 Map p92, A4

A snug spot to get stuffed (literally), kooky, attitude-free Bankeråt is decorated with taxidermic animals in outlandish get-ups – yes, there's even a ram in period costume. The man behind it all is local artist Filip V Jensen. But is it art? Debate this, and the mouth-shaped urinals, over a local craft beer (a much better choice than the very average wines). Best of all, part of the bar's profits go to helping sponsor kids. (☏33 93 69 88; www.bankeraat.dk; Ahlefeldtsgade 27; ⏱9.30am-11pm Mon & Tue, to midnight Wed-Fri, 10.30am-midnight Sat, 10.30am-8pm Sun; 🛜; 🚌37, 5C, 350S, 🅼Nørrebro, 🆂Nørrebro)

Shopping

Stine Goya   FASHION & ACCESSORIES

10 🔒 Map p92, D4

The winner of numerous prestigious design awards, Stine Goya is one of Denmark's hottest names in women's fashion. What makes her collections unique is the ability to marry clean Nordic simplicity with quirky details. Memorable recent offerings include silky 'oversized' frocks printed with painted human faces, svelte bee-print jumpsuits and a canary-yellow bomber jacket featuring contemporary local artwork. Not cheap but highly collectable. (☏32 17 10 00; www.stinegoya.com; Gothersgade 58; ⏱11am-6pm Mon-Fri, to 4pm Sat; 🚌350S, 🅼Kongens Nytorv)

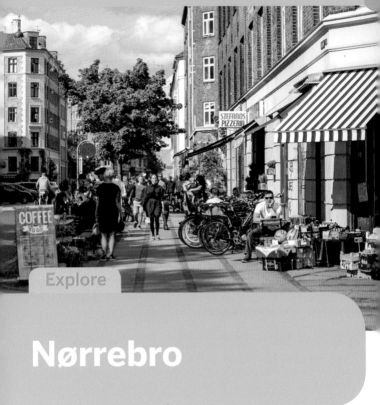

Explore

Nørrebro

Gritty Nørrebro subverts the Nordic stereotype with its dense, sexy funk of art-clad 19th-century tenements, multicultural crowds and thronging cafes and bars. Despite being home to Assistens Kirkegård – the final resting place of Hans Christian Andersen – this corner of the city is less about sights and more about independent craft stores and galleries, craft beers and kaleidoscopic street life.

The Sights in a Day

☀️ Ease into the Nørrebro groove at artisanal bakery and cafe **Mirabelle** (p101). Next, explore the fashion boutiques and antique shops on Guldbergsgade, Elmegade and Ravnsborggade. If it's Saturday, treasure-hunt at longstanding flea market **Nørrebro Loppemarked** (p105).

☀️ Escape to **Assistens Kirkegård** (p99) and seek out the graves of writer Hans Christian Andersen and Golden Age artists Christoffer Wilhelm Eckersberg and Christen Købke. The cemetery is one of the city's most inviting green spaces, and a popular sunbathing spot in the summer. Lunch on regional grub at **Manfreds og Vin** (p102), hop the Jægersborggade's booty of artisan studios and fashion boutiques, and down a local craft beer at **Mikkeller & Friends** (p102).

🌙 As evening descends, dive into good-time **Kassen** (p104) for happy-hour cocktail specials, then get those fingers dirty at **Oysters & Grill** (p101) – always a good idea to book ahead. If you feel like kicking on, head to Ravnsborggade, a street packed with bustling bars. Among them is the supremely sultry **Kind of Blue** (p104).

💜 **Best of Copenhagen**

Eating
Oysters & Grill (p101)

Drinking
Brus (p102)

Mikkeller & Friends (p102)

Entertainment
Rust (p103)

Getting There

🚌 **Bus** Routes 5C and 350S connect the city centre to Nørrebro. Both routes run along Nørrebrogade, Nørrebro's main thoroughfare.

200 m
0.1 miles

Tagensvej

Panum
Institutet

Blegdamsvej

Læssøesgade

13

Sankt Hans Gade

Ravnsborggade

12

Tandlægeskolen

Nørre Allé

Møllegade

Ahornsgade

Fælledvej

Nørrebrogade

11

Edis Rodes Vej

Guldbergsgade

10

Jagtvejsgade

Egegade

14

Baggesensgade

Fensmarksgade

Guldbergsgade

Peter Fabers Gade

Møllegade

Birkegade

Emegade

Stengade

Griffenfeldsgade

Sjællandsgade

Meinungsgade

Nørrebrogade

Kapelvej

Rålards

Prinsesse Charlottes Gade

2

17

Kapelvej

Zoologisk
Museum (900m)

Nørrebros
Runddel

Nørrebrogade

Assistens
Kirkegård

1

Nørrebros
Runddel (under
construction)

Hans Tavsens Gade

Struenseegade

Nørrebroparken

Julius Bloms Gade

Husumgade

Jægersborggade

Jagtvej

Kronborggade

Hørsholmsgade

Rantzausgade

Stengade

Bjelkes Allé

16

4

15

9

8

6

For reviews see

⊙	Sights	p99
⊗	Eating	p99
⊕	Drinking	p102

OLL0815/GETTY IMAGES ©

Grave of Hans Christian Andersen, Assistens Kirkegård

Sights

Assistens Kirkegård CEMETERY

1  Map p98, B3

You'll find some of Denmark's most celebrated citizens at this famous cemetery, including philosopher Søren Kierkegaard, physicist Niels Bohr, author Hans Christian Andersen and artists Jens Juel, Christen Købke and CW Eckersberg. It's a wonderfully atmospheric place to wander around – as much a park and garden as it is a graveyard. A good place to start is at the main entrance on Kapelvej, where you can usually find fold-out maps of the cemetery and its notable burial sites. (📞35 37 19 17; http://assistens.dk; Kapelvej 4, Nørrebro; ⏰7am-10pm Apr-Sep, to 7pm Oct-Mar; 🚌5C, 8A)

Eating

Oysters & Grill SEAFOOD $$

2 🍴 Map p98, C2

Finger-licking surf and turf is what you get at this rocking, unpretentious neighbourhood favourite, complete with kitsch vinyl tablecloths and a fun, casual vibe. The shellfish is fantastically fresh and, unlike most

Top Tip

It might sound macabre, but historic cemetery Assistens Kirkegård is a popular picnic and sunbathing spot in the warmer months. Graced with leafy, tranquil nooks, it's a blissful spot to spend a lazy afternoon reading a good book or simply contemplating the beauty of life… and maybe cheese.

places, ordered by weight, which means you don't need to pick at measly servings. Meat lovers won't to be disappointed either, with cuts that are lustfully succulent. (📞70 20 61 71; www.cofoco.dk/da/restauranter/oysters-and-grill; Sjællandsgade 1B; mains 165-245kr; ⏱5.30pm-midnight; 🚇5C)

Bæst
ITALIAN $$

3 🍴 Map p98, D2

Owned by powerhouse Italo-Scandi chef Christian Puglisi, Bæst remains hot years after its 2014 launch. Charcuterie, cheese and competent wood-fired pizzas are the drawcards here. Much of the produce is organic, and both the commendable charcuterie and hand-stretched mozzarella are made upstairs (the latter made using jersey milk from Bæest's own farm). To fully appreciate its repertoire, opt for the sharing menu (small/large 375/450kr). (📞35 35 04 63; www.baest.dk; Guldbergsgade 29; pizzas 85-150kr; ⏱5-10.30pm; 📶; 🚇3A, 5C)

Relæ
NEW NORDIC $$$

4 🍴 Map p98, A2

Established by prolific chef Christian Puglisi, Relæ was one of the first restaurants in town to offer superlative New Nordic cooking without all the designer fanfare. One Michelin star later, it remains a low-fuss place, where diners set their own table, pour their own wine and swoon over soul-lifting dishes focused on seasonality, simplicity and (mostly) organic produce. Book ahead. (📞36 96 66 09; www.restaurant-relae.dk; Jægersborggade 41; 4-/7-course menu 475/895kr; ⏱5-10pm Tue-Sat, also noon-1.30pm Fri & Sat; 🚇8A, 5C)

Mirabelle
CAFE $

5 🍴 Map p98, D2

Decked out with bold geometric floor tiles, artisan bakery-cafe Mirabelle is owned by Michelin-lauded chef Christian Puglisi, who also owns popular restaurant Bæst next door. It's a slick, contemporary spot for made-from-scratch pastries, simple breakfast bites like eggs Benedict, and a short menu of Italo-centric lunch and dinner dishes, including house-made charcuterie, cheeses and organic-flour pasta. Good coffee to boot. (📞35 35 47 24; http://mirabelle-bakery.dk; Guldbergsgade 29; pastries from 28kr, sandwiches 65kr, lunch & dinner dishes 115-175kr; ⏱7am-10pm; 📶; 🚇3A, 5C)

Understand
Eco Capital

While some Western governments continue to debate the veracity of climate-change science, Denmark gets on with innovative, sustainable business. Indeed, the Danish capital is well on its way to becoming the world's first carbon neutral capital by 2025.

Green Mobility
Implementation of the CPH 2025 Climate Plan's focus areas – energy consumption, energy production, green mobility and city-administration initiatives – is visible across the city. Two new metro lines will open in 2019, including a 15.5km-long city-circle route. Copenhagen public transport agency Movia predicts that its opening will see up to 34 million passengers ditch buses for the metro annually. In the meantime, hundreds of city buses have been upgraded with special air filters that cut pollution by 95%.

Denmark's capital is crisscrossed by over 400km of safe, connected bike paths, and even the traffic lights are programmed to give cyclists precedence in peak hour. Less than 30% of local households own a car and, for the first time in 2016, the number of bikes trumped the number of cars in the city centre.

Ditching the Dirt
Ready to remind Copenhageners of the pressing nature of environmental matters is the city's new waste-to-energy plant, Amager Bakke. Designed by local architecture firm Bjarke Ingels Group (BIG), the world's cleanest incineration plant includes a chimney that blows out smoke rings (made of ecofriendly water vapour) for each 250kg of carbon dioxide released into the atmosphere. It's a novel reminder of the importance of reducing carbon emissions.

For Copenhagen, this also involves a hand from its harbour. City energy utility company HOFOR uses an innovative district cooling system that utilises local seawater to provide cooling services to businesses in central Copenhagen. The system saves around 70% of the energy used by traditional air-conditioning systems. Copenhagen harbour itself is an environmental success story: the once heavily polluted waterway is now clean enough for swimming.

Q Local Life

Manfreds og Vin

Convivial **Manfreds og Vin** (Map p98, A1; 36 96 65 93; www.manfreds.dk; Jægersborggade 4; small plates 75-90kr; 7-course tasting menu 285kr; noon-3.30pm & 5-10pm; ; ; 8A) is the ideal local bistro, with passionate staffers, boutique natural wines and a regularly changing menu that favours organic produce (most from the restaurant's own farm) cooked simply and sensationally. Swoon over nuanced, gorgeously textured dishes like grilled spring onion served with pistachio puree, crunchy breadcrumbs and salted egg yolk. If you're hungry and curious, opt for the good-value seven-dish menu.

Møller

BREAKFAST $

7 Map p98, B1

Møller is a cosy and rustic all-day-breakfast haven with a focus on quality local ingredients. Eggs, meats, cheeses, breads and more are offered individually so you can create your own meal according to your tastes – a sort of tapas-style breakfast. The house-made sourdough bread, fresh nuggets with mayo, and the half avocado filled with crumbed almonds, chilli and crème fraiche are especially delicious. (31 50 51 00; www.kaffeogkoek-ken.dk; Nørrebrogade 160; breakfast dishes 18-46kr; 9am-4pm; ; 5C)

Drinking

Brus

MICROBREWERY

7 Map p98, D2

What was once a locomotive factory is now a huge, sleek, hip brewpub. The world-renowned microbrewery behind it is To Øl, and the bar's 30-plus taps offer a rotating selection of To Øl standards and small-batch specials, as well as eight on-tap cocktails. The bar-keeps are affable and happy to let you sample different options before you commit. (75 22 22 00; http://tapperiet-brus.dk; Guldbergsgade 29F; 3pm-midnight Mon-Thu, noon-3am Fri & Sat, noon-midnight Sun; ; 5C)

Mikkeller & Friends

MICROBREWERY

8 Map p98, A1

Looking suitably cool with its tur-quoise floors and pale ribbed wood, Mikkeller & Friends is a joint venture of the Mikkeller and To Øl brewer-ies. Beer geeks go gaga over the 40 artisan draft beers and circa 200 bottled varieties, which might include a chipotle porter or an imperial stout aged in tequila barrels. Limited snacks include dried gourmet sausage and cheese. (35 83 10 20; www.mikkeller.dk/ location/mikkeller-friends; Stefansgade 35; 2pm-midnight Sun-Wed, to 2am Thu & Fri, noon-2am Sat; ; 5C, 8A)

CAMILLA STEPHAN/MIKKELLER & FRIENDS, COPENHAGEN ©

Mikeller & Friends

Coffee Collective

COFFEE

9 Map p98, A2

Copenhagen's most prolific microro-astery, Coffee Collective has helped revolutionise the city's coffee culture in recent years. Head in for rich, complex cups of caffeinated magic. The baristas are passionate about their single-origin beans and the venue itself sits at one end of creative Jægersborggade in Nørrebro. There are three other outlets, including at gourmet food market Torvehallerne KBH (p90) and in **Frederiksberg** (📞 60 15 15 25; https://coffeecollective.dk; Godthåbsvej 34b, Frederiksberg; ⏰ 7.30am-6pm Mon-Fri, from 9am Sat, from 10am Sun). (www.coffeecollective.dk; Jægersborggade 57,

Nørrebro; ⏰ 7am-8pm Mon-Fri, 8am-7pm Sat & Sun; 🚌 8A)

Rust

CLUB

10 Map p98, D3

A smashing, multilevel place attract-ing one of the largest, coolest, most relaxed crowds in Copenhagen. Live acts focus on alternative or upcoming indie rock, hip-hop or electronica. At 11pm, the venue transforms into a club, with local and international DJs pumping out anything from classic hip-hop to electro, house and more. (📞 35 24 52 00; www.rust.dk; Guldbergsgade 8, Nørrebro; ⏰ hours vary, club usually 8.30pm-5am Fri & Sat; 📶; 🚌 3A, 5C, 350S)

Kassen BAR

11 🚇 Map p98, D4

Loud, sticky Kassen sends livers packing with its dirt-cheap drinks and happy-hour specials (80kr cocktails, anyone?). Guzzle unlimited drinks on Wednesdays for 250kr, with two-for-one deals running the rest of the week: all night Thursdays, 4pm to 10pm Fridays and 8pm to 10pm Saturday. Cocktail choices are stock-standard and a little sweet, but think of the change in your pocket. (📞42 57 22 00; http://kassen.dk; Nørrebrogade 18B, Nørrebro; ⏰8pm-late Wed, Thu & Sat, from 4pm Fri; 🚌5C)

Kind of Blue BAR

12 🚇 Map p98, E3

Chandeliers, heady perfume and walls painted a hypnotic 1950s blue: the spirit of the Deep South runs deep at intimate Kind of Blue. Named after the Miles Davis album, it's never short of a late-night hipster crowd, kicking back porters and drinking in owner Claus' personal collection of soul-stirring jazz, blues and folk. You'll find it on Nørrebro's bar-packed Ravnsborggade. (📞26 35 10 56; www.kindofblue.dk; Ravnsborggade 17, Nørrebro; ⏰4pm-midnight Mon-Wed, to 2am Thu-Sat; 🛜; 🚌5A, 350S)

Nørrebro Bryghus BREWERY

13 🚇 Map p98, E3

This now-classic brewery kickstarted the microbrewing craze more than a decade ago. While its in-house restaurant serves a decent lunchtime burger as well as fancier New Nordic dishes in the evening, head here for the beers, including the brewery's organic draught beer and a string of fantastic bottled options, from pale and brown ales to 'The Evil', a malty, subtly smokey imperial porter. (📞35 30 05 30; www.noerrebrobryghus.dk; Ryesgade 3, Nørrebro; ⏰noon-11pm Mon-Thu, to 1am Fri & Sat, to 10pm Sun; 🚌3A, 5C, 350S)

P2 by Malbeck WINE BAR

14 🚇 Map p98, D3

A lush wine bar adorned with plants, crisp timber and golden pendant lamps, P2 is a refreshing spot for a buzzing, grown-up vino session. Wines by the glass usually start at a democratic 60kr or 65kr and the list normally includes a number of biodynamic options from around the world. Bites are of the tapas variety. (📞32 21 52 15; Birkegade 2, Nørrebrø; ⏰4pm-midnight Mon-Thu, to 1am Fri & Sat; 🛜; 🚌3A, 5C, 350S)

Shopping

Vanishing Point HANDICRAFTS

15 🔒 Map p98, A2

On trendy Jægersborggade, Vanishing Point is a contemporary craft shop and studio showcasing quirky ceramics, unique jewellery, handmade knits and quilts, as well as engaging, limited-edition prints. Most items are created on-site, while some are the result of a collaboration with non-profits around the world. The aim: to inspire a sustainable and playful

Understand
Vilhelm Dahlerup & Dronning Louises Bro

It is said that no single architect has contributed to Copenhagen's current look as much as Vilhelm Dahlerup (1836–1907). The city's leading architect of the late 19th century, Dahlerup borrowed from a broad spectrum of European Renaissance influences. His Historicist style of architecture shines especially bright in Ny Carlsberg Glyptotek and the glorious Det Kongelige Teater, two exceptional works in a long list of buildings that also include the Hotel d'Angleterre, Pantomime Theatre at Tivoli Gardens, Carlsberg Brewery and Statens Museum for Kunst.

The influence of the French Empire Style is palpable in Dahlerup's **Dronning Louises Bro** (Map p98, E4; 🚌5C, Ⓜ Nørreport, Ⓢ Nørreport), the bridge connecting central Copenhagen to Nørrebro. Dating from 1887, its namesake is Queen Louise, wife of Christian IX. The current crossing succeeds two earlier versions: a wooden bridge built in the 16th century and a combined bridge-dam constructed a century later. In the evening, the bridge offers a prime-time view of Nørrebrø's famous neon lights; the best-loved of them is the Irma hen, laying electric eggs since 1953.

---

lifestyle through nature, traditional craft techniques and humour. (📞25 13 47 55; www.vanishing-point.dk; Jægersborggade 45, Nørrebro; ⊙11am-5.30pm Mon-Fri, to 6pm Sat, to 3pm Sun; 🚌8A)

Gågron! HOMEWARES
16 🅰 Map p98, A2

Gågron! peddles design-literate products with a conscience. The focus is on natural fibers and sustainable, recycled and upcycled materials, transformed into simple, stylish products for everyday use. Stock up on everything from kooky animal-shaped cutting boards and stylish cedar-wood serving trays to aprons and toiletry bags made with organic cotton. (📞42 45 07 72; www.gagron.dk; Jægersborggade

48, Nørrebro; ⊙11am-5.30pm Mon-Fri, 10am-3.30pm Sat, 11am-3pm Sun; 🚌8A)

Nørrebro Loppemarked MARKET
17 🅰 Map p98, C2

Running alongside the wall of Assistens Kirkegård on Nørrebrogade, this is Denmark's longest flea market, with over 300 metres of stalls. Head in early and rummage through the junk for quirky antiques and jewellery, old LPs and art, not to mention the odd Royal Copenhagen porcelain piece. It runs every Saturday from early April to the end of October. (www.berling-samlerting.dk/32693948; Nørrebrogade, Nørrebro; ⊙8am-3pm Sat Apr-Oct; 🚌5C, 8A, 350S)

Local Life
Østerbro

Getting There

🚌 **Bus** Route 1A connects central Copenhagen to Trianglen, the heart of Østerbro. From Vesterbro, Frederiksberg and Nørrebro, route 3A also reaches Trianglen.

Detractors might call it 'white bread' and boring, but salubrious Østerbro serves up some satisfying urban surprises, including heritage-listed architecture and a cinema-turned-design Valhalla. The neighbourhood's name means 'East Gate', a reference to the city's old eastern entrance. These days, it's an area best known for its resident media stars, academics, and slew of foreign embassies.

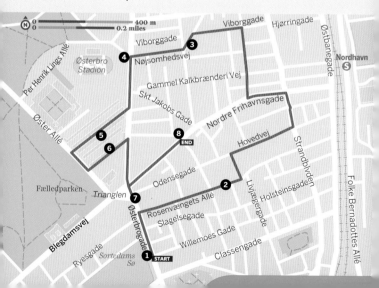

❶ Sortedams Sø

Sortedams Sø (Black Dam Lake) is the most northerly of Copenhagen's trio of central lakes. It's popular with joggers and flâneurs, and a is good spot to sit and reflect.

❷ Rosenvænget

Bordered by Rosenvængets Sideallé, Strandboulevarden, Holsteinsgade and Nordre Frihavnsgade, Rosenvænget is the city's oldest suburban development, established in the mid-19th-century. Rosenvaengets Allé 46 was designed by Vilhelm Dahlerup, creator of Ny Carlsberg Glyptotek.

❸ Pixie

Strung with colourful lights, boho cafe **Pixie** (☎39 30 03 05; www.cafepixie.dk; Løgstørgade 2; dishes 55-195kr; ⏰8am-midnight Mon-Thu, to 4am Fri & Sat, 10am-11pm Sun; 📶; 🚇1A) looks straight off the streets of Buenos Aires. Inside it's a hyggelig affair, with mismatching furniture and candlelight. If the weather's on your side, grab a table on the leafy square.

❹ Øbro-Hallen

Inspired by the baths of ancient Rome, beautiful **Øbro-Hallen** (☎82 20 51 50; http://teambade.kk.dk/indhold/oebrohallen; Gunnar Nu Hansens Plads 3; adult/child 40/20kr; ⏰7am-8pm Mon, Tue & Fri, from 8am Wed, from 6.30am Thu, 9am-3pm Sat & Sun; 🚼; 🚇1A) is Denmark's oldest indoor public pool complex (1929–31). It's also one of its most beautiful, awash with natural light from its elegant glass ceiling.

❺ Brumleby

Celebrated Danish writers Martin Andersen Nexø (*Pelle the Conqueror*) and Peter Høeg (*Miss Smilla's Feeling for Snow*) have both called Brumleby home. A heritage-listed combo of yellow-and-white row-housing and cosy gardens, the residential enclave was built to better house the poor after the 1853 cholera epidemic.

❻ Olufsvej

Technicolor Olufsvej is lined with 19th-century workers' abodes in a multitude of shades. These days, the properties are home to a number of well-known journalists.

❼ Normann Copenhagen

Sprawling **Normann Copenhagen** (☎35 27 05 40; www.normann-copenhagen.com; Østerbrogade 70; ⏰10am-6pm Mon-Fri, to 4pm Sat; 🚇1A, 14) bursts with musthave design objects, from statement bowls and glassware to furniture, lighting and cushions. The space was once a cinema.

❽ Fischer

Another reformed local is **Fischer** (☎35 42 39 64; www.hosfischer.dk; Victor Borges Plads 12; lunch mains 129-189kr, dinner mains 239kr; ⏰8am-midnight Mon-Fri, from 10am Sat & Sun; 📶; 🚇3A), a former workingman's bar turned neighbourly trattoria. It makes sense that the Italian grub is so good, given that owner and head chef David Fischer worked the kitchen at Rome's Michelinstarred La Pergola.

Explore

Vesterbro

Once best known for butchers and hookers, Vesterbro is now the epicentre of Copenhagen cool. The neighbourhood's hottest corner remains Kødbyen (Meat City), a still-functioning Meatpacking District laced with buzzing eateries, bars, galleries and music venues. Istedgade mixes porn shops with vintage boutiques and ethnic groceries, while further north lies continental Værnedamsvej.

The Sights in a Day

☀ Like Nørrebro, Vesterbro is more about the vibe than blockbuster tourist sights. Start with breakfast or brunch at **Granola** (p110), one of Copenhagen's best-loved cafes. It's right on Værnedamsvej so once you're done, shop-hop the street. Further west on adjoining Vesterbrogade is **Designer Zoo** (p119), a solid spot for local design.

☀ When the hunger pangs kick in, trawl the stalls at indoor street-food hub **WestMarket** (p115), which peddles everything from classic Danish comfort grub to tacos, bao and Thai. Continue south to Istedgade, where you could easily spend the rest of the afternoon hunting down interesting fashion and knick-knacks or just kicking back at a cafe for a spot of people-watching.

☾ Once you're done, hit post-industrial Kødbyen for drinks and dinner. Top eating choices here include **Paté Paté** (p114) and **Kødbyens Fiskebar** (p115). If you feel like hanging around, jump into **Mesteren & Lærlingen** (p118). Alternatively, sip craft beers at cult-status **Mikkeller Bar** (p118) or smash cocktails at easy-to-miss cocktail bar **Lidkoeb** (p117).

For a local's day in Vesterbro, see p110.

🔍 Local Life
Continental Værnedamsvej

♥ Best of Copenhagen

Eating
WestMarket (p115)

Kødbyens Fiskebar (p115)

Hija de Sanchez (p116)

Drinking
Lidkoeb (p117)

Shopping
Designer Zoo (p119)

Getting There

🚌 **Bus** Routes 6A and 26 run along Vesterbrogade to Frederiksberg Have. Route 9A runs along Gammel Kongevej, connecting Vesterbro to Slotsholmen and Christianshavn.

🚆 **Train** Kødbyen lies 500m south-west of Central Station.

Local Life
Continental Værnedamsvej

Copenhagers have a soft spot for Værnedamsvej, a sassy little strip they commonly compare to the side streets of Paris. Gallic or not, it is one of Vesterbro's most appealing pockets, dotted with specialist cheese and wine shops, cafes and bistros, petite boutiques and an unmistakably easy, local vibe. Some shops close on the weekends, so head in during the week for the full experience.

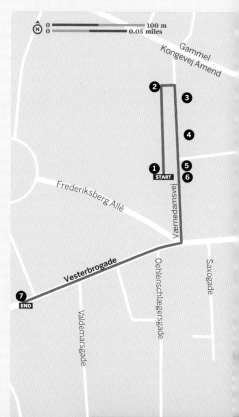

❶ Granola

Granola (☏40 82 41 20; www.granola.dk; lunch 80-165kr, dinner mains 145-220kr; ☉7am-midnight Mon-Fri, 9am-midnight Sat, 9am-4pm Sun; ☐9A, 26, 31, 71) is a staple of Copenhagen's breakfast and weekend brunch scene, with a cute general store-inspired fitout. While the menu doesn't pack any extraordinary punches, it does offer reliable comfort grub, from morning oatmeal, croque monsieur and pancakes, to lunch and dinner bistro staples like steak frites, Head in early on weekends.

❷ Juuls Vin og Spiritus

Vintage wine shop **Juuls Vin og Spiritus** (☏ 33 31 13 29; www.juuls.dk; ⏲ 9am-5.30pm Mon-Thu, to 7pm Fri, to 5pm Sat; 🚌 6A, 9A, 31) sells some thirst-inducing drops, not to mention an impressive range of whiskies. Fine local choices include spicy, fruity Brøndum Kummenaquavit, as well as organic snaps from Hven, a tiny Swedish island located in the Øresund.

❸ Falernum

Worn floorboards and chairs, bottled-lined shelves and soothing tunes give wine bar **Falernum** (Map p112, D1; ☏ 33 22 30 89; www.falernum.dk; ⏲ noon-midnight Sun-Thu, to 2am Fri & Sat; 📶; 🚌 6A, 9A, 31) a deliciously moody air. You'll find around 40 wines by the glass alone, as well as boutique beers, coffee and a simple, seasonal menu of sharing plates like osso buco with roasted artichokes and onions, as well as cheeses and charcuterie.

❹ Samsøe & Samsøe

Originating from the Latin Quarter and now based in Nørrebro, **Samsøe & Samsøe** (☏ 35 28 51 02; www.samsoe.com; ⏲ 10am-6pm Mon-Thu, to 7pm Fri, to 5pm Sat, 11am-4pm; 🚌 6A, 9A, 31) is well known for its contemporary threads for guys and girls. This is a label not afraid of unique patterns, colour and detailing, and the range includes supremely comfortable sweat tops, tees

and denim, as well as sharper shirts, jackets, frocks and outerwear. The store also stocks selected items from guest labels.

❺ Dora

Christian Lacroix notebooks, quilted laptop covers, hand-painted lava-stone cheese: design shop **Dora** (☏ 32 21 33 57; www.shopdora.dk; ⏲ 10am-6pm Mon-Fri, to 4pm Sat, noon-4pm Sun; 🚌 6A, 9A, 31) likes to keep things highly idiosyncratic, with harder-to-find objects for any room and any occasion. Look out for cool local stuff from brands like Hay and LuckyBoySunday.

❻ Playtype

Font freaks will go gaga at **Playtype** (☏ 60 40 69 14; www.playtype.com; ⏲ noon-6pm Mon-Fri, 11am-3pm Sat; 🚌 6A, 9A, 26), an online type foundry with its own real-life, hard-copy shop. The theme is Danish-designed fonts, showcased as letters, numbers and symbols on everything from posters, notebooks and postcards, to crew necks, raincoats, laptop covers and mugs.

❼ Prag

Just around the corner from Værnedamsvej is **Prag** (☏ 33 79 00 50; www.pragcopenhagen.com; ⏲ 10am-6pm Mon-Fri, to 5pm Sat, noon-5pm Sun; 🚌 3A, 6A). It's one of Copenhagen's funkiest consignment stores, peddling an eclectic booty of threads and accessories for both women and men. Need a frou-frou frock or tutu? A polka-dot bow tie? Maybe a vintage kimono? Chance are you'll find it here.

For reviews see

◉ Sights		p114
✖ Eating		p114
🖰 Drinking		p117
★ Entertainment		p119
🔒 Shopping		p119

0   200 m
0   0.1 miles

Gammel Kongevej Amend

Frederiksberg Allé

Sankt Thomas Plads

Frederiksberg Allé

Værnedamsvej

Kingosgade

FREDERIKSBERG

Vesterbrogade

4 ✖

Oehlenschlægersgade

Valdemarsgade

Hennik Ibsens Vej

Platanvej

Vesterbrogade

Amerikavej

Tøndergade

Sundevedsgade

Hedebygade

Enghavevej

Matthæusgade

🔒✖9
19

Vesterfælledvej

Frederiksstadsgade

Carstensgade

Rejsbygade

Lyrskovgade

18 ★

Haderslevgade

Istedgade

🔒20

Saxogade

Enghave Plads (under construction)

Ⓜ

Enghaveparken

Enghave Plads

Flensborggade

Valdemarsgade

Oehlenschlægersgade

Ny Carlsberg Vej

Haderslevgade

Vesterfælledvej

Alsgade

Slesvigsgade

Enghavevej

Sonder Blvd

Angelgade

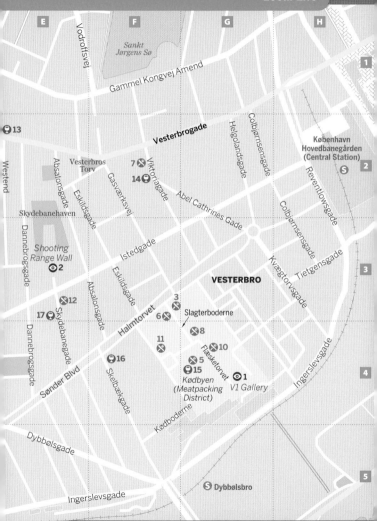

Sights

V1 Gallery
GALLERY

1 ◉ Map p112, G4

Part of the Kødbyen (Vesterbro's 'Meatpacking District'), V1 is one of Copenhagen's most progressive art galleries. Cast your eye on fresh work from both emerging and established local and foreign artists. Some of the world's hottest names in street and graffiti art have exhibited here, from Britain's Banksy to the USA's Todd James and Lydia Fong (aka Barry McGee). (☑33 31 03 21; www.v1gallery.com; Flæsketorvet 69-71; admission free; ⊘noon-6pm Wed-Fri, to 4pm Sat during exhibitions; 🚌1A, 10, 14, Ⓢ Dybbølsbro)

Top Tip

Street Art

Both Vesterbro and Frederiksberg are home to some huge, spectacular street-art murals. Many of these cover the side walls of semidetached apartment buildings. In Vesterbro, honourable mentions go to Irish artist Conor Harrington's period piece at Tullingsgade 21, Brooklynite Maya Hayuk's geometric statement at Saxogade 7, Belgian artist Roa's furry critters at Gasværksvej 34 and Chinese artist DALeast's giant bird at Oehlenschlægersgade 76. In Frederiksberg, don't miss homegrown Martin Bigum's storybook work at Falkoner Allé 30.

Shooting Range Wall
HISTORIC SITE

2 ◉ Map p112, E3

In a cul-de-sac off Istedgade is this imposing red-brick wall, its gate leading to the delightful Skydebanehaven (Shooting Range Gardens). While it might look medieval, the wall dates back to 1887. At the time, this was the site of the Royal Copenhagen Shooting Society and the wall was built to protect locals from stray bullets. The club's target was parrot shaped, leading to the popular Danish saying 'You've shot the parrot there', used to refer to someone's good fortune.

Today, the playground pays tribute to this past with a parrot-shaped slide. (Istedgade 68-80; 🚼; 🚌10, 14, Ⓢ København H)

Eating

Paté Paté
INTERNATIONAL $$

3 🍴 Map p112, F3

This pâté factory-turned-restaurant/wine bar gives a modern twist to Euro classics. The regularly changing menu is designed for sharing, with smaller dishes like organic Danish burrata with salted courgette, spring onions, chilli, basil and walnuts, or veal tartare with harissa, mustard-pickled shallots and dukkah. Hip and bustling, yet refreshingly convivial, bonus extras include clued-in staff, a diverse wine list, and solo-diner-friendly bar seating. (☑39 69 55 57; www.patepate.dk; Slagterboderne 1; small dishes 95-150kr, 7/9-plate tasting menu 325/385kr; ⊘9am-10pm Mon-Thu, 9am-11pm Fri, 11am-11pm Sat; 🛜; 🚌10, 14)

ANNAPURNA MELLOR/GETTY IMAGES ©

Meatpacking district

WestMarket

MARKET $

4 Map p112, C2

From dodgy shopping arcade to cool street-food hub, WestMarket peddles grub from all corners of the globe: from ramen, bao and lobster rolls to risotto, bubbling pizza and tapas. For a Scandi experience, hit **Kød & Bajer** (☎30 54 60 88; www.koedogbajer.dk; Vesterbrogade 97, Stall C12t; ⊗11am-9pm; 📵6A) for harder-to-find Nordic craft beers and snacks like dried moose, bear and elk sausages, then settle down at **Gros** (☎60 45 11 02; www.groshverdagskost. dk; Vesterbrogade 97, Stall C6; meals 98kr; ⊗11am-9pm; 🛜🖋; 📵6A) for a modern take on retro Danish dining classics. (☎70 50 00 05; www.westmarket.dk;

Vesterbrogade 97, Vesterbro; meals from 50kr; ⊗bakeries & coffee shops 8am-7pm, food stalls 10am-10pm; 🛜🚻; 📵6A)

Kødbyens Fiskebar

SEAFOOD $$$

5 Map p112, G4

Concrete floors, industrial tiling and a 1000-litre aquarium meet impeccable seafood at this ever-popular, buzzy haunt, slap bang in Vesterbro's trendy Kødbyen (Meatpacking District). Ditch the mains for three or four starters. Standouts include the oysters and lobster with beer meringue, as well as the dainty, delicate razor clams, served on a crisp rice-paper 'shell'. (☎32 15 56 56; www.fiskebaren.dk; Flæsketorvet 100; mains 195-275kr; ⊗5.30pm-midnight Mon-Thu,

11.30am-2am Fri & Sat, 11.30am-midnight Sun; 📶; 🚇10, 14, **S** Dybbølsbro)

Hija de Sanchez   MEXICAN $

6 🍴 Map p112, F3

Hija de Sanchez serves up fresh, authentic tacos in the Meatpacking District. Expect three rotating varieties daily, from traditional choices like *carnitas* and *al pastor* to 'El Paul' – crispy fish skin with gooseberry salsa. There's always a vegetarian option, as well as homemade Mexican beverages like *tepache* (fermented pineapple juice). Chicago-native chef-owner Rosio Sánchez hails from renowned restaurant Noma, ie serious culinary cred. (📞31 18 52 03; www.hijadesanchez.dk; Slagterboderne 8; 3 tacos 100kr; ⏰11am-8pm Mon-Thu, to 10pm Fri & Sat, to 6pm Sun; 🚇1A, 10, 14, **S** Dybbølsbro)

Øl & Brød   DANISH $$

7 🍴 Map p112, F2

Modernist Danish furniture and a muted palette of greys and greens offer the perfect backdrop to high-end, contemporary lunchtime smørrebrød. Raise your glass of (craft) beer to beautiful combinations like smoked mackerel with scrambled egg and chives or dill-pickled herring with potatoes and mustard. The dinner menu offers revisited Danish mains; think whole butter-fried flounder with parsley sauce and potatoes. (📞33 31 44 22; www.ologbrod.dk; Viktoriagade 6; smørrebrød 85-165kr, dinner mains 150-250kr; ⏰noon-5pm Tue & Wed, to 10pm Thu & Sun, to 11pm Fri & Sat Apr-Dec, reduced hours Jan-Mar; 📶; 🚇6A, 9A, 10, 14, 26, **S** København H)

Nose2Tail   DANISH $$$

8 🍴 Map p112, G4

Candlelit industrial tiles, old Danish crockery, crooked old photos: this former basement factory finds its muse in the Danish bars of yesteryear. Here, every part of the animal is used to cook up honest, rustic, made-from-scratch fare. The surf-turf menu is short, seasonal and ethical: the meat is from welfare-minded farms and the produce is mainly organic and from small, local producers. (📞33 93 50 45; https://nose2tail.dk; Flæsketorvet 13; mains 250-375kr, 4-course tasting menu 450kr; ⏰6pm-1am Mon-Sat; 📶; 🚇10, 14)

Pony   NEW NORDIC $$

9 🍴 Map p112, A3

This is the cheaper, bistro spin-off of Copenhagen's Michelin-starred Kadeau. While the New Nordic grub here is simpler, it's no less nuanced and seasonal; think cured brill with gooseberries and dried brill roe, or roasted wolffish with summer cabbage, black cabbage, nasturtium and crispy grains. The on-point wines are organic and from smaller producers, and the vibe intimate and convivial.

Book ahead, especially on Friday and Saturday. (📞33 22 10 00; www.ponykbh. dk; Vesterbrogade 135; 2/3/4-course menu 325/425/485kr; ⏰5.30-10pm Tue-Sun; 🚇6A)

WarPigs

BARBECUE **$$**

10 Map p112, G4

Loud, rocking WarPigs satiates carnivores with lusty, American-style barbecue from Europe's biggest meat smokers (capable of smoking up to two tons of meat a day!). Order at the counter, where you can mix and match meats and sides to create a personalised feed. There's also a kicking selection of beers brewed in-house; the place doubles as a brewpub part-owned by local microbrewery **Mikkeller**.

Tommi's Burger Joint

BURGERS **$**

11 Map p112, F4

Hip Iceland export Tommi's Burger Joint sits in the heart of the trendy Meatpacking District. The place is small and packed (consider avoiding peak times), with old-school posters on the walls and music on the stereo. The menu is short, simple and competent: three juicy burgers, a trio of fries and frosty milkshakes to wash it all down. (☎ 33 31 34 34; www.burgerjoint.dk/kodbyen; Høkerboderne 21-23, Vesterbro; burgers 79-84kr; ◷ 11am-9pm Mon-Wed, to 10pm Thu-Sun; ☐ 1A, 10, 14, **S** Dybbølsbro)

Siciliansk Is

ICE CREAM **$**

12 Map p112, E3

Honing their skills in Sicily, gelato meisters Michael and David churn out Copenhagen's (dare we say Denmark's) best gelato. Lick yourself out on smooth, naturally flavoured options like strawberry, Sicilian blood orange and coconut. For a surprisingly smashing combo, try the *lakrids* (liquorice) with the Sicilian mandarin. *Buonissimo!* (☎ 30 22 30 89; http://sicilianskis.dk; Skydebanegade 3, Vesterbro; ice cream from 25kr; ◷ noon-9pm mid-May–Aug, 1-6pm Apr–mid-May & Sep; ☐ 10, 14)

Drinking

Lidkoeb

COCKTAIL BAR

13 Map p112, E2

Lidkoeb loves a game of hide-and-seek: follow the 'Lidkoeb' signs into the second, light-strung courtyard. Once found, this top-tier cocktail lounge rewards with passionate barkeeps and clever, seasonal libations. Slip into a Børge Mogensen chair and toast to Danish ingenuity with Nordic bar bites and seasonal drinks like the Freja's Champagne: a gin-based concoction with muddled fresh ginger, lemon and maraschino liqueur.

Extras include a dedicated whisky bar upstairs, open Friday and Saturday nights only. (☎ 33 11 20 10; www.lidkoeb.dk; Vesterbrogade 72B, Vesterbro; ◷ 4pm-2am Mon-Sat, from 8pm Sun; ☎; ☐ 6A, 26)

Mikkeller Bar

BAR

14 Map p112, F2

Low-slung lights, milk-green floors and 20 brews on tap: cool, cult-status Mikkeller flies the flag for craft beer, its rotating cast of suds including Mikkeller's own acclaimed creations and guest drops from microbreweries from

Local Life

Dyrehaven

Once a spit-and-sawdust working-class bar (the vinyl booths tell the story), **Dyrehaven** (Map 113, E5; www.dyrehavenkbh.dk; Sønder Blvd 72, Vesterbro; breakfast 30-140kr, lunch 70-95kr, dinner mains 120-195kr; ⏱8.30am-2am Mon-Fri, from 9am Sat & Sun; 🛜; 🚌1A, 10, 14) is now a second home for Vesterbro's cool, young bohemians. Squeeze into your skinny jeans and join them for cheap drinks, simple tasty grub and DJ-spun tunes on Friday and Saturday nights (summer excepted).

around the globe. Expect anything from tequila-barrel-aged stouts to yuzu-infused fruit beers. The bottled offerings are equally inspired, with cheese and snacks to soak up the foamy goodness. (📞33 31 04 15; http://mikkeller.dk; Viktoriagade 8B-C; ⏱1pm-1am Sun-Wed, to 2am Thu & Fri, noon-2am Sat; 🛜; 🚌6A, 9A, 10, 14, 26, Ⓢ København H)

Mesteren & Lærlingen   BAR

15 🍷 Map p112, G4

In a previous life, Mesteren & Lærlingen was a slaughterhouse bodega. These days it's one of Copenhagen's in-the-know drinking holes, its tiled walls packing in an affable indie crowd of trucker caps and skinny jeans. Squeeze in and sip good spirits

(including a decent mezcal selection) to DJ-spun soul, reggae, hip-hop and dance hall. Wi-fi is available if you ask politely. (www.facebook.com/Mesteren-Lærlingen-215687798449433; Flæsketorvet 86; ⏱8pm-3am Wed & Thu, to 3.30am Fri & Sat; 🛜)

Fermentoren   CRAFT BEER

16 🍷 Map p112, F4

Serious local beer fans flock to this cosy, candlelit basement bar. Its 24 taps pour an ever-changing cast of interesting craft brews, both traditional and edgy. Look out for local brews from the likes of Evil Twin, Ghost and Gamma, as well as Fermentoren's own pale ale. Staff are extremely knowledgeable, offering expert advice without the attitude. (📞23 90 86 77; http://fermentoren.com; Halmtorvet 29C; ⏱3pm-midnight Mon-Wed, 2pm-1am Thu & Fri, 2pm-2am Sat, 2pm-midnight Sun; 🛜; 🚌1A, 10, 14, Ⓢ Dybbølsbro)

Sort Kaffe & Vinyl   CAFE

17 🍷 Map p112, E3

This skinny little cafe/record store combo is a second home for Vesterbro's coffee cognoscenti. Join them for velvety espresso, hunt down that limited-edition Blaxploitation LP, or score a prized pavement seat and eye up the eye-candy regulars. (📞61 70 33 49; Skydebanegade 4; ⏱8am-9pm Mon-Fri, from 9am Sat & Sun Jul & Aug, 8am-7pm Mon-Fri, 9am-7pm Sat, 9am-6pm Sun rest of year; 🚌10, 14)

Entertainment

Vega Live
LIVE MUSIC

18 ⭐ Map p112, B4

The daddy of Copenhagen's live-music venues, Vega hosts everyone from big-name rock, pop, blues and jazz acts to underground indie, hip-hop and electro up-and-comers. Gigs take place on either the main stage (Store Vega), small stage (Lille Vega) or the ground-floor Ideal Bar. Performance times vary; check the website. (☑ 33 25 70 11; www.vega.dk; Enghavevej 40; 📶; 🚌 3A, 10, 14, Ⓢ Dybbølsbro)

Shopping

Designer Zoo
DESIGN

19 🔒 Map p112, A3

If you find yourself in Vesterbro – and you should – make sure to drop into this supercool design hub. A store, gallery and workshop complex in one (the staff are actual designers and artisans), it's a platform for independent Danish design talent. Scan both floors for locally made limited-edition objects spanning jewellery, soft furnishings and furniture to ceramics and glassware. (☑ 33 24 94 93; www.dzoo.dk; Vesterbrogade 137; 🕙 10am-6pm Mon-Fri, to 3pm Sat; 🚌 6A)

Local Life
Cykelslangen

Two of the Danes' greatest passions – design and cycling – meet in spectacular fashion with **Cykelslangen** (Cycle Snake). Designed by local architects Dissing + Weitling, the 235-metre-long cycling path evokes a slender ribbon, its gently curving form contrasting dramatically against the area's block-like architecture. The elevated path winds its way from Bryggebro west to Fisketorvet Shopping Centre, delivering a cycling experience that's nothing short of whimsical. To reach the path on public transport, catch bus 34 to Fisketorvet Shopping Centre. The best way is on a bike, as Cykelslangen is only accessible to cyclists.

Kyoto
FASHION & ACCESSORIES

20 🔒 Map p112, D4

Unisex, multi-brand Kyoto pulls cool hunters with its awesome edits of mostly Nordic labels: think hardy S.N.S. Herning knits, Wrench Monkey shirts, Norse Project tees, Acne Studios denim, as well as Libertine Libertine and Rodebjer frocks. International interlopers include French labels A.P.C. and Kitsuné, while the cast of well-chosen accessories include statement sneakers, fragrances and slinky leather wallets. (☑ 33 31 66 36; http://kyoto.dk; Istedgade 95; 🕙 10am-6pm Mon-Thu, to 7pm Fri, to 5pm Sat; 🚌 10, 14)

Local Life
Frederiksberg

Aspiring Copenhagers dream of a Frederiksberg address. Located directly west of Vesterbro, it's a moneyed district, laced with fin-de-siècle architecture, neighbourly bistros and leafy residential streets. It's here that you'll find the landscaped elegance of Frederiksberg Have and the architecturally notable Copenhagen Zoo, as well as one of Copenhagen's finest flea markets.

Getting There

🚌 **Bus** Routes 9A and 31 run past Frederiksberg Rådhus. Route 8A runs along the eastern edge of Frederiksberg Have. Routes 6A and 72 run along the park's southern flank (including the zoo). Route 26 stops near Carlsberg Brewery.

Ⓜ **Metro** Frederiksberg station lies 300m north of Frederiksberg Rådhus.

Ⓢ **S-Train** Carlsberg station lies 400m east of Carlsberg Brewery.

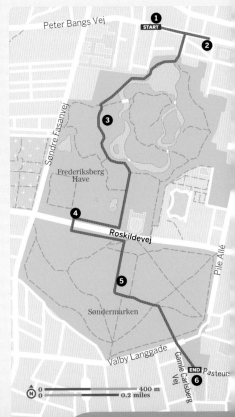

1 Sokkelund

Classic **Sokkelund** (📞38 10 64 00; http://
cafe-sokkelund.dk; Smallegade 36E; mains
165-259kr; ⏱8am-11pm Mon-Fri, 9.30am-
11pm Sat, 9.30am-10pm Sun; 📶; 🚌8A, 9A,
31, 74) is the quintessential neighbourhood brasserie, kitted out with leather
banquettes, newspapers on hooks
and handsome waiters in crisp white
shirts. Breakfast, lunch, or dinner, join
the steady stream of regulars for flex-
ible bistro bites, including some of the
juiciest burgers in town.

2 Frederiksberg Loppetorv

If it's Saturday, scour cult-status flea
market **Frederiksberg Loppetorv**
(Frederiksberg Flea Market; Smallegade,
Frederiksberg Rådhus; ⏱9am-3pm Sat Apr–
mid-Oct; 🚌8A, 9A, 31). The neighbourhood's affluence is reflected in the
quality of the goods, and seasoned
treasure hunters head in early for the
best finds. There's usually plenty of
local and international fashion, with
the odd Danish design collectable in
the mix.

3 Frederiksberg Have

Romantic **Frederiksberg Have** (Frederiksberg Runddel; ⏱7am-11pm mid-Jun–
mid-Aug, to 10pm May–mid-Jun & mid-late
Aug, reduced hours rest of year; 🚌6A, 8A, 71,
72) woos with its lakes and woodlands.
Look out for the Chinese summer-
house pavilion, built in 1803 by court
architect Andreas Kirkerup. Overlook-
ing the park is Frederiksborg Slot, a
former royal palace, now home to the
Royal Danish Military Academy.

4 Copenhagen Zoo

Perched on Frederiksberg (Frederik's
Hill), **Copenhagen Zoo** (📞72 20 02
00; www.zoo.dk; Roskildevej 32; adult/child
180/100kr; ⏱10am-6pm Jun & mid-late Aug,
to 8pm Jul–mid-Aug, reduced hours rest of
year; 🚌6A, 72) rumbles with more than
2500 of nature's lovelies. Its elephant
enclosure was designed by English
architect Sir Norman Foster, and the
newer Arctic Ring enclosure allows
visitors to walk right through the
polar-bear pool.

5 Cisternerne

Below Søndermarken Park lurks
Copenhagen's 19th-century water
reservoir. These days it's best known as
Cisternerne (📞30 73 80 32; www.cistern-
erne.dk; Søndermarken; adult/child 60kr/free;
⏱vary; 🚌6A, 72), one of Copenhagen's
most unusual art spaces. The gallery
runs one major exhibition every year –
check the website.

6 Carlsberg Brewery

Carlsberg Brewery was designed
by architect Vilhelm Dahlerup. The
brewery's **visitors center** (📞33 27 12 82;
www.visitcarlsberg.dk; Gamle Carlsberg Vej 11,
Vesterbro; adult/child 100/70kr; ⏱10am-
8pm May-Sep, to 5pm rest of year; 🚌1A, 26,
Ⓢ Carlsberg) explores the history of
Danish beer from 1370 BC, leading
you past antique copper vats and the
brewery's famous Jutland dray horses.
The self-guided tour ends at the bar,
where two free beers await. A new
visitors centre is due to open in 2017.

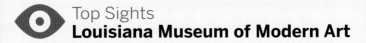

Top Sights
Louisiana Museum of Modern Art

Getting There

S **S-Train** Louisiana lies in the town of Humlebæk, 30km north of central Copenhagen. From Central Station and Nørreport, S-trains run regularly to Humlebæk station. From here, the museum is a 1.5km signposted walk along Gammel Strandvej.

Even if you don't have a consuming passion for modern art, Denmark's outstanding Louisiana should be high on your 'to do' list. It's a striking modernist gallery, made up of four huge wings, which stretch across a sculpture-filled park, burrowing down into the hillside and nosing out again to wink at the sea (and Sweden).

Sculpture park, Louisiana Museum of Modern Art

www.louisiana.dk

Gammel Strandvej 13, Humlebæk

adult/student/child 125/110kr/free

⏱11am-10pm Tue-Fri, to 6pm Sat & Sun

Permanent Collection

The museum's permanent collection, mainly post-war paintings and graphic art, covers everything from constructivism, CoBrA movement artists and minimalist art, to abstract expressionism, pop art and staged photography. Pablo Picasso, Francis Bacon and Alberto Giacometti are some of the international luminaries you'll come across inside, while prominent Danish artists include Asger Jorn, Carl-Henning Pedersen, Robert Jacobsen and Richard Mortensen.

Architecture

The Danish architects Vilhelm Wohlert and Jørgen Bo spent several months walking around the grounds before deciding on their design for Louisiana. The result would be one the country's finest examples of modernist architecture, a series of horizontal, light-washed buildings in harmony with their natural surroundings. The museum's three original buildings – completed in 1958 and known as the North Wing – are now accompanied by subsequent extensions. The seats in the Concert Hall are the work of the late designer Poul Kjaerholm.

Sculpture Garden

With views across the deep-blue Øresund to Sweden, Louisiana's arresting grounds are peppered with sculptures from some of the world's most venerated artists. You'll find works from the likes of Max Ernst, Louise Bourgeois, Joan Miró, Henry Moore and Jean Arp, each one positioned to interact with the environment surrounding it. Site-specific works include George Trakas' *Self Passage* and Richard Serra's *The Gate in the Gorge*.

☑ Top Tips

▶ Check the museum website for upcoming events, which include regular evening art lectures and live music.

▶ If you have kids in tow, head to the Children's Wing, where they can create their own masterpieces inspired by the gallery's exhibitions.

✖ Take a Break

With its large sunny terrace and sea views, Louisiana's cultured cafe is a fabulous spot for lunch or a reviving coffee.

The Best of
Copenhagen

Copenhagen's Best Walks

A Slotsholmen Saunter 126

Nørrebro Soul 128

Copenhagen's Best...

Museums & Galleries 130

Shopping 132

Eating 134

Drinking 136

Entertainment 137

Hygge 138

For Free 139

Tours 140

For Kids 141

Architecture 142

Design 143

Festivals & Events 144

Best Walks
A Slotsholmen Saunter

The Walk

Looks can be very deceiving. While Slotsholmen may look small on a city map, this compact island is Denmark's powerhouse. It's right here that politicians debate policy, that supreme-court judges set precedents, and that the Queen plays host with the most. This easy meander will have you crossing Copenhagen's most romantic bridge, scanning the city from its tallest tower and relaxing in a harbour-turned-secret library garden. Intrigued? You should be.

Start Marmorbroen; 🚍1A, 2A, 9A, 26, 37 to Stormbroen

Finish Ved Stranden 10; 🚍1A, 2A, 9A, 26, 37 to Christiansborg Slotsplads

Length 2km; 1.5 hours

Take a Break

Sip and graze at one of Copenhagen's best wine bars, **Ved Stranden 10** (p51).

WIBOWO RUSLI/GETTY IMAGES ©

Black Diamond (p41) interior

❶ Marmorbroen

Designed by Nicolai Eigtved, the **Marble Bridge** is one of Copenhagen's rococo highlights. Completed in 1745, it dates from the original Christiansborg Slot, which went up in flames in 1794.

❷ Christiansborg Ridebane

The **Riding Ground complex** also survived the fire, offering a glimpse of the palace's original baroque style. The square's only decoration is Vilhelm Bissen's 19th-century equestrian statue of Frederik VII.

❸ Christiansborg Slot Tower

Head into Christiansborg Slot through the main entrance to climb the palace **tower** (p38). Fans of the Danish TV drama Borgen will know that it's right here that Birgitte's mentor Bent Sejrø encourages her to fight for the role of statsminister.

❹ Det Kongelige Biblioteks Have

The open archways of the red-brick building facing Christiansborg

Slot's southern side lead to the charming **Royal Library Garden**. The garden sits on Christian IV's old naval port, Tøjhushavnen. The towering fountain sculpture is an ode to the written word. Created by Mogens Møller, it shoots water every hour on the hour.

❺ Det Kongelige Bibliotek

Just south of the garden, **Det Kongelige Bibliotek** (p41) is home to the **Black Diamond**, the library's world-renowned extension. Completed in 1999, the building's sleek, somber façade is clad in black granite sourced from Zimbabwe and polished in Italy. Head to the upper floors for a spectacular view of the atrium.

❻ Børsen

Head north along the waterfront, then turn left onto Slotsholmsgade to reach 17th-century **Børsen** (p42). Copenhagen's old stock exchange, it was originally flanked by water on three sides and topped with a lead roof. The lead was used to make cannonballs during the Swedish occupation in 1658–59.

❼ Ved Stranden 10

From Børsen, cross Holmens Bro and treat yourself to a well-earned tipple at **Ved Stranden 10** (p51), a well-versed wine bar with canalside seating in the summer and snug, Danish-designer interiors.

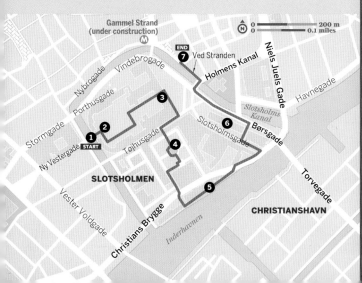

Best Walks
Nørrebro Soul

🏃 The Walk

Nørrebro is Copenhagen's creative heart, a multiethnic enclave splashed with quirky parks and street art, intriguing workshops and studios, as well as the city's most beautiful eternal resting place. So tie up those sneakers and hit the pavement for red squares and bulls, giant birds and tankers, and a shady street turned good.

Start Superkilen; 🚍 5A to Nørrebrogade

Finish Jægersborggade; 🚍 8A to Jagtvej

Length 2km; 1.5 hours

🍴 Take a Break

End your saunter with superlative coffee at **Coffee Collective** (p102).

Superkilen

❶ Superkilen

Created by local architecture studio Bjarke Ingels Group, Berlin-based landscape architects Topotek1 and Danish art group Superflex, the 1km-long park **Superkilen** is a hyperplayful ode to the area's multicultural fabric, with Russian neon signs, Ghanaian bollards, even a Spanish bull.

❷ Basco5 Mural

Head east along Mimersgade, turning left into Bragesgade. On the side of number 35 is a **street art mural** by Copenhagen artist Nils Blishen, better known as Basco5. Birds, bearded men and a round, cartoonish style are all trademarks of the artist's work.

❸ BaNanna Park

Turn right into Nannasgade and walk 250m to oil-refinery-turned-playground **BaNanna Park**. Its striking gateway is a 14-metre-high climbing wall, popular with eye-candy locals and open to all (BYO climbing equipment).

❹ Odinsgade Murals

Step right into Råd-mandsgade, left into Mimersgade, and right again into Thorsgade. Two blocks ahead is **Odinsgade**. The whimsical **mural** on the side of number 17 is by Simon Hjermind Jensen, Anne Sofie Madsen and Claus Frederiksen. The adjacent tanker mural uses existing architectural features to dramatic effect.

❺ Assistens Kirkegård

At Jagvej, turn right, and continue to hallowed **Assistens Kirkegård** (p99). In 2013 the cemetery created a 75-sq-metre burial plot for the city's homeless, complete with a bronze sculpture by artist Leif Sylvester. Each day, eccentric local Captain Irishman collects flowers for the plot.

❻ Jægersborggade

Directly opposite Assistens Kirkegård, Jægersborggade is a vibrant hub of craft studios, boutiques and eateries. At no 45, **Vanishing Point** (p104) showcases quirky local ceramics, jewellery, handmade knits, quilts and engaging, limited-edition prints, much of it made on site. At No 48, **Gågron!** (p105) peddles design-literate everyday products with a conscience.

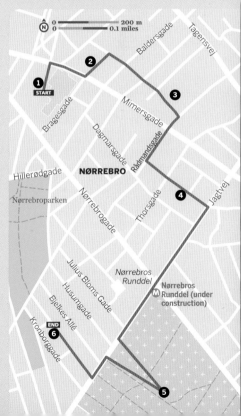

Best
Museums & Galleries

Copenhagen is packed with engaging museums and galleries, from the epic to the eclectic. Together they house a seemingly endless array of cultural treasures, from ancient tomb wares and sacrificial bodies to dazzling swords and jewels, iconic modernist design and envelope-pushing contemporary installations from Denmark and beyond. Strap on some comfy kicks and hit the ground running.

KIM NILSSON/NY CARLSBERG GLYPTOTEK ©

☑ Top Tip

▶ If you plan on blitzing the museums, consider purchasing the **Copenhagen Card** (p150) which offers free entry to 79 museums and attractions, as well as free public transport. Sights covered include Rosenborg Slot, Nationalmuseet and Ny Carlsberg Glyptotek.

Plan Your Visit

Many museums and galleries close at least one day a week, usually on Monday. Some stay open late one or more nights a week, often on Wednesday or Thursday. While Nationalmuseet, Statens Museum for Kunst and Davids Samling are always free, some museums – among them Ny Carlsberg Glyptotek and Thorvaldsens Museum – offer free admission once a week, often on Wednesday or Sunday.

Park Museums

Statens Museum for Kunst, Rosenborg Slot, Davids Samling, Hirschsprung, Statens Naturhistoriske Museum (including Geologisk Museum) and Cinemateket together form the Parkmuseerne (www.parkmuseerne.dk) district. A combination ticket (Dkr195) covers all venues and includes a 10% discount on publications at Davids Samling and a free cinema ticket at Cinemateket.

Best for History

Nationalmuseet The country's entire biography under one roof. (p28)

Rosenborg Slot Royal bling in Christian IV's Renaissance summer pad. (p84)

Louisiana Museum of Modern Art (p122)

Ruinerne under Christiansborg The ruins of Copenhagen's earliest fortress and castle. (p37)

Designmuseum Danmark Explore the roots of Danish design. (p60)

De Kongelige Stalde An equine affair of carriages, uniforms and riding equipment at the Royal Stables. (p42)

Tøjhusmuseet Analyse historical battles at the Royal Danish Arsenal Museum. (p43)

Best Art Museums

Statens Museum for Kunst Denmark's preeminent art collection spans medieval to modern. (p88)

Louisiana World-class masterpieces with an aside of modernist architecture. (p122)

Ny Carlsberg Glyptotek Egyptian and Mediterranean antiquities plus Impressionist art. (p31)

Thorvaldsens Museum Denmark's first museum building and a shrine to the nation's greatest sculptor. (p41)

Best Lesser-known Treasures

Davids Samling A neoclassical apartment graced with Eastern and Western treasures. (p93)

Hirschsprung An elegant repository of 19th- and 20th-century Danish art. (p94)

Dansk Jødisk Museum Jewry heritage in a space designed by architect Daniel Libeskind. (p42)

Best Contemporary Art Galleries

Kunsthal Charlottenborg One of Europe's largest venues for modern talent from around the globe. (p65)

Kunstforeningen GL Stand A canalside showcase of forward-thinking local and foreign works. (p48)

V1 Gallery Edgy exhibitions in Vesterbro's vibrant Meatpacking District. (p114)

Cisternerne A former underground reservoir turned dramatic installation space. (p121)

Best
Shopping

What Copenhagen's shopping portfolio lacks in size it more than makes up for with quality and individuality. The city is Scandinavia's capital of cool, with no shortage of locally designed and crafted must-haves to respark your spending fire. Good buys that are easy enough to carry home include unique streetwear and higher-end fashion, ceramics, glassware, jewellery and textiles. Ready, set, shop.

Where to Shop

Strøget offers mostly generic fashion chains, with the more upmarket options at its eastern end (Østergade). Amagertorv is home to flagship stores for Royal Copenhagen, George Jensen and design behemoth Illums Bolighus. More High St chains line Købmagergade, with the hippest Nordic fashion stores concentrated in the streets east of Købmagergade and north of Østergade (including Gammel Mønt, Grønnegade and Møntergade). A handful of vintage stores dot the Latin Quarter, with some quirky, higher-end fashion stops on Krystalgade.

North of Nyhavn, salubrious Bredgade offers exclusive art and antiques. For more affordable bric-a-brac, vintage jewellery and kitschy objects, scour Ravnsborggade in Nørrebro or explore Nørrebro Loppemarked, the neighbourhood's seasonal Saturday flea market. Nørrebro is also home to Elmegade and Jægersborggade, two streets pimped with independent shops. Vesterbro is another good bet for independent fashion and homewares, with most of the offerings on and around Istedgade and Værndamsvej.

NON-EXCLUSIVE/GETTY IMAGES ©

☑ Top Tip

▶ Citizens from countries outside the EU can claim a VAT refund on goods as they leave the EU (as long as they spend a minimum of 300kr per shop and the shop participates in one of the refund schemes). Get the shop to fill in a refund form, then present it, together with your passport, receipts and purchases, at the airport upon departure.

Best Women's Threads

Stine Goya Playful, individualistic outfits from Denmark's hottest independent designer. (p95)

Designer Zoo storefront

Baum und Pferdgarten
Bold, colourful, higher-end collections from a Danish duo. (p56)

Storm Harder-to-find labels, accessories and gifts in a unisex concept store. (p56)

Best for Men's Threads

NN07 High-quality, pared-back threads and accessories fusing Nordic and Japanese aesthetics. (p56)

Wood Wood Cult-status concept store stocking in-house streetwear, plus guest labels, footwear, eyewear and fragrances. (p57)

Samsøe & Samsøe Super-cool, comfy casualwear from Samsøe as well as guest labels. (p111)

Best for Interior Design

Hay House Contemporary furniture, furnishings and gifts from new-school Scandi talent. (p55)

Stilleben Gorgeous ceramics, textiles, jewellery and gifts from emerging and forward-thinking local designers. (p55)

Designer Zoo An eclectic range of homewares, furniture and threads sold by actual artisans. (p119)

Illums Bolighus Four floors of design for every room in your house. (p55)

Gourmet Treats

Torvehallerne KBH A celebrated food market heaving with goods for the pantry and cellar. (p90)

Juuls Vin og Spiritus Stock the cellar with Nordic akvavits, gins and more. (p111)

Local Gifts & Souvenirs

Posterland Awesome selection of posters, including retro ads for Danish beer, transport, cities and more. (p56)

Designmuseum Danmark Cool, easy-to-carry gifts, from local jewellery and Nordic cookbooks to statement-making socks. (p60)

Best
Eating

Beneath Copenhagen's galaxy of Michelin stars is a growing number of hotspots serving innovative contemporary Danish fare at affordable prices. The international food scene is also lifting its game, with a spate of new places serving authentic dishes like pho, ramen and tacos made using top-notch produce. Keeping them company are veritable city institutions serving classic Danish fare, including smørrebrød.

SARAH COGHILL / LONELY PLANET ©

Old-school Flavours

Reindeer moss and hay-smoked quail eggs may be the norm on New Nordic menus, but traditional Danish tables are a heartier affair. Pork (*flæskor svinekød*) shines in comfort-food favourite *frikadeller*, fried minced-pork meatballs commonly served with boiled potatoes and red cabbage. Equally iconic is the majestic *stjerneskud*. Literally 'shooting star', it's a belt-busting combination of both steamed and fried fish fillets, topped with smoked salmon, shrimp and caviar, and served on buttered bread.

The Sweet Stuff

Ironically, what is known as a 'Danish pastry' abroad is known to the Danes as a *wienerbrød* (Viennese bread). As legend has it, the naming of the pastry can be traced to a Danish baker who moved to Austria in the 18th century, where he perfected the treats of flaky, butter-laden pastry. Not that Denmark's pastry selection ends there. Other famous treats include *kanelsnegle* (cinnamon snail), a scroll sometimes laced with thick, gooey chocolate.

☑ Top Tips

▶ Reserve a table at popular restaurants, especially later in the week. Many of them offer easy online reservations.

▶ Copenhageners are not Mediterraneans, meaning that if you like to eat late, you'll have trouble finding a place to accommodate you after about 10pm.

Traditional Danish

Schønnemann An epic repertoire of smørrebrød good enough for Michelin-starred chefs. (p50)

Café Halvvejen Generous serves of hearty grub in a timbered time machine. (p51)

Outdoor food stalls, Kødbyen, Vesterbro

Orangeriet Lunchtime smørrebrød in a romantic garden setting. (p85)

Kanal Caféen Salt-of-the-earth staff, epic Danish platters and a canalside location. (p32)

Modern Danish

Kadeau Breathtaking degustations bursting with creativity. (p78)

Höst Sophisticated New Nordic at approachable prices. (p94)

108 Locavore sharing plates at Noma's more casual spinoff. (p78)

Bror Impressive, sharply executed dishes from a pair of Noma alumni. (p32)

Restaurant Mes Subtle foreign twists and whimsical presentation. (p32)

Pluto Seasonal, honest grub in a buzzing, friendly space. (p94)

Asian Flavours

District Tonkin Authentic *bánh mì* (Vietnamese baguettes) and northern Vietnamese bites. (p66)

The Market Intriguing pan-Asian flavours in a slinky space. (p50)

Seafood

Oysters & Grill Spectacular oysters, shellfish and more at a convivial, casual favourite. (p101)

Kødbyens Fiskebar Creative, high-end sharing plates in a buzzy industrial setting. (p115)

Cheap Eats

WestMarket An arcade packed with a globe's worth of quality street food. (p115)

Hija de Sanchez Real-deal, high-quality tacos from a Noma alumnus. (p116)

Tommi's Burger Joint Lusty burgers in the Meatpacking District. (p117)

DØP Premium hot dogs made with 100% organic ingredients. (p51)

Best
Drinking

Copenhagen is packed with a diverse range of drinking options. Vibrant drinking areas include Vesterbro's Kødbyen (Meatpacking District), Istedgade and the northern end of Viktoriagade; Nørrebro's Ravnsborggade, Elmegade, Sankt Hans Torv and Jægersborggade; and the historic Latin Quarter. On a sunny day, there's always touristic Nyhavn, although prices are higher and the handful of great spots are just off it.

SARAH COGHILL/LONELY PLANET ©

Where to Drink

Vibrant drinking areas include Vesterbro's Kødbyen (Meatpacking District), Istedgade and the northern end of Viktoriagade; Nørrebro's Ravnsborggade, Elmegade, Sankt Hans Torv and Jægersborggade; and the historic Latin Quarter. On a sunny day, there's always touristic Nyhavn, although prices are higher and the handful of great spots are just off it.

For Cocktails

Ruby Meticulous, made-from-scratch cocktails at one of the world's Top 50 bars. (p52)

Lidkoeb Beautiful libations in a hidden location right off Vesterbrogade. (p117)

1105 A dark, sleek city-centre cocktail den for grown-ups. (p52)

For Wine

Ved Stranden 10 Knowledgeable staff pouring unusual drops. (p51)

Mother Wine Boutique Italian vino, late-week aperitivo and fair prices. (p52)

Nebbiolo Trendy Italian enoteca with top drops just off Nyhavn. (p68)

Den Vandrette Natural wines and summertime harbourside tables. (p68)

☑ Nyhavn For Less

▸ Skip Nyhavn's touristy canalside bars and buy your beers and wine cheaper at seasonal convenience store Turs Havneproviant, just off the northern side of the canal at Lille Strandstræde 3. Stocked up, sit right by the canal and toast to the simple things in life. It's legal.

For Craft Beer

Brus Twenty-four rotating beers on tap, including standout local brews. (p102)

Mikkeller & Friends Craft brews, plus Belgian-style beers in a back bar. (p102)

Best
Entertainment

Copenhagen's entertainment offerings are wide, varied and sophisticated. On any given night choices will include ballet, opera, theatre, clubbing and live tunes spanning indie and blues to pop. The city has a world-renowned jazz scene, with numerous jazz clubs drawing top talent. Note: many nightspots don't get the party started until 11pm or midnight.

SARAH COGHILL/LONELY PLANET ©

Live Music & DJs

Vega Live Three venues in one, serving up an alphabet of genres. (p119)

Rust A classic spot for indie rock, pop, hip-hop and electronica. (p103)

Culture Box Electronic music spun by A-list local and global DJs. (p95)

Loppen Raw, feverish, alternative acts in a scruffy Christiania warehouse. (p75)

Jazz & Blues

Jazzhouse A bumper line-up of both local and visiting jazz masters. (p53)

Jazzhus Montmartre A veteran jazz peddler, with decent pre-show dining. (p53)

Mojo Moody nightly tunes spanning blues

to soul, plus an affable, welcoming vibe. (p33)

Performing Arts

Det Kongelige Teater Encore-worthy ballet and opera in Copenhagen's most opulent period theatre. (p68)

Skuespilhuset Contemporary home of the Royal Danish Theatre, with classic and modern productions. (p69)

Operaen Sterling opera in a showstopping harbourside landmark. (p81)

For Cinephiles

Cinemateket Quality independent cinema, including bimonthly Danish film classics. (p55)

Grand Teatret A vintage movie house with a weakness for Euro movies.

☑ **Top Tip**

▶ Located at the main Tivoli Gardens entrance, **Tivoli Box Office** (📞 33 15 10 01; Vesterbrogade 3; ⏰ 10am-10.45 Sun-Thu, to 11.45pm Fri & Sat summer, 10am-6pm Mon-Fri rest of year) not only sells Tivoli performance tickets, it's also an agent for **BilletNet** (📞 70 15 65 65; www.billetnet.dk), which sells tickets for concerts, theatre, comedy, sporting events and music festivals.

(www.grandteatret.dk; Mikkel Bryggers Gade 8; ⏰ 11am-10.30pm; 📶; 🚌 12, 14, 26, 33; Ⓢ København H)

Best
Hygge

While it might be a little unusual to call a feeling a city highlight, in the case of Danish *hygge*, we heartily recommend that you grab a piece of the action.

Hygge: 101

What is *hygge*? How do you achieve it? And just how does it feel? Light some candles, pour a warming cup of coffee, and read on. While there is really no equivalent in English, *hygge* loosely refers to a sense of friendly, warm companionship of a kind fostered when Danes gather together in groups of two or more. The participants don't even have to be friends (indeed, you might only have just met), but if the conversation flows – avoiding potentially divisive topics like politics and the best way to pickle a herring – the bonhomie blossoms, and toasts are raised before an open fire (or, at the very least, some tealights), you are probably coming close.

SARAH COGHILL/LONELY PLANET ©

☑ Top Tip

▶ Danish *hygge* reaches fever pitch in December, when twinkling lights, flowing *gløgg* (mulled wine) and Tivoli Garden's famous Christmas market crank up the cosiness and camaraderie.

For Old-School Hygge

Tivoli Gardens A mood-lifting jumble of carnival rides, twinkling lights and old-fashioned charm. (p24)

Café Halvvejen Heart Danish dishes, spirit-lifting snaps and nostalgic surrounds. (p51)

La Glace Snuggle up with hot tea and a luscious slice of walnut cake. (p51)

For Hip Hygge

Manfreds og Vin A snug neighbourhood eatery with beautiful nosh and wine. (p102)

Øl & Brød A modern take on classic Danish design, food, beer and hospitality. (p116)

Lidkoeb Sheepskin, candles and a festive courtyard set a *hyggelig* scene for superlative libations. (p117)

Bastard Café Hipsters and geeks relive their wonder years over board games and drinks. (p52)

Best
For Free

While Copenhagen is hardly a bargain destination, the city does spoil the well-informed with free thrills, including some of its most impressive sights. Some are always free, while others are free on specific days of the week. Best of all the city's compact size means it's easy enough to save money on transport, keeping costs lower and your spirits higher.

SARAH COGHILL/LONELY PLANET ©

Best Always-Free Museums

Davids Samling A dazzling booty of Islamic treasures, and European paintings and applied arts. (p93)

Best Sometimes Free Museums

Ny Carlsberg Glyptotek From Egyptian tombs to French impressionists, an eclectic cultural hoard that's free on Tuesdays. (p31)

Thorvaldsens Museum Wednesdays cost nada at this ode to Denmark's most accomplished sculptor. (p41)

Nikolaj Kunsthal The contemporary art exhibitions inside this former church are free on Wednesdays. (p49)

Best Free Experiences

Assistens Kirkegård Enjoy one-on-one time with some of Denmark's most illustrious historical figures. (p99)

Islands Brygge Havne-badet Work it, flaunt it or just get it wet at Copenhagen's hottest harbour pool complex. (http://teambade.kk.dk/indhold/havnebade-0; Islands Brygge; admission free; ⊙24hr Jun-Sep, 🚻; 🚌5C, 12, Ⓜ Islands Brygge)

Christiania Soak up the sights, sounds and scents of Copenhagen's most unconventional neighbourhood. (p72)

Christiansborg Slot Tower The million-dollar view from Copenhagen's tallest tower is complimentary. (p38)

☑ Top Tip

▶ **Copenhagen Free Walking Tours** (www.copenhagen freewalkingtours. dk) runs a three-hour Grand Tour of Copenhagen daily at 10am, 11pm and 3pm, departing from outside Rådhus. A 90-minute Classical Copenhagen Tour departs daily at noon. A 90-minute Christianshavn tour departs daily at 4pm from Højbro Plads. Tours are technically free though a tip is expected.

Botanisk Have Wander through the largest collection of living plants in Denmark. (p93)

Best
Tours

Best Overview Tours

Netto-Bådene (📞 32 54 41 02; www.havnerundfart. dk; adult/child 40/15kr; 🕐 tours 2-5 per hour, 10am-7pm Jul & Aug, reduced hours rest of year) The cheapest of Copenhagen's harbour and canal tours, with embarkation points at Holmens Kirke and Nyhavn.

Canal Tours Copenhagen (📞 32 96 30 00; www. stromma.dk; adult/child 80/40kr; 🕐 9.30am-9pm late Jun–mid-Aug, reduced hours rest of year; 👬) Highly popular one-hour harbour and canal tours departing from Nyhavn and Ved Stranden.

Copenhagen City Sightseeing (📞 32 96 30 00; www.citysightseeing.dk; tickets adult/child from 158/79kr; 🕐 departures every 30-60min, 9.30am-4.30pm daily late Apr–mid-Sep, shorter hours & routes rest of year) A hop-on, hop-off bus with three routes to choose from. The two-day 'Bus & Boat combo' also covers Canal Tours Copenhagen.

Best Active Tours

Kayak Republic (📞 22 88 49 89; www.kayakrepublic.dk; 1/2/3hr rental 175/275/375kr, 2hr guided tour 395kr; 🕐 10am-9pm Jun-Aug, reduced hours rest of year) Two-hour tours along the city's canals, as well as less-frequent, three-hour tours focused on Nordic food or architecture. Located just beside Christian IV's Bro.

Bike Copenhagen With Mike (📞 26 39 56 88; www.bikecopenhagenwithmike.dk; per person 299kr) Idiosyncratic three-hour cycling tours of Copenhagen, departing from Sankt Peders Stræde 47 in the city centre. Seasonal and private tours are also available; see the website.

Running Tours Copenhagen (📞 50 59 17 29; www.runningtours.dk; 1-2 people 350kr, each additional person 100kr) Run or jog your way through the city and its history. Themes include Grand Tour, Night Run and Pub Run, with tours commencing in Rådhuspladsen.

QUADRIGA IMAGES / LOOK-FOTO / GETTY IMAGES ©

Best Themed Tours

Nordic Noir Tours (www.nordicnoirtours.com; per person 150kr, if booked online 100kr; 🕐 The Killing/The Bridge tour 4pm Sat, pre-booked Borgen tour 2pm Sat) Retrace the steps of your favourite Nordic TV characters from *Borgen*, *The Bridge* and *The Killing* on these 90-minute location walking tours. Tours depart from Vesterport S-train station.

CPH:cool (📞 50 58 28 24; www.cphcool.dk; tour 1-6 people from 1650kr) Two- and two-and-a-half-hour insider walking tours with themes like shopping, architecture, design, gastronomy and beer. Tours leave from outside the Copenhagen Visitors Centre.

Best
For Kids

GIANNI MARCHETTI/GETTY IMAGES ©

Copenhagen seems tailor-made for little ones. And we're not just talking about its world-famous, centrally located amusement park, Tivoli Gardens either. We're talking about free entry for kids at most museums, engaging cultural institutions with special family activities, child-friendly parks and beaches, and a transport system that actually considers prams.

For Artistic Inspiration

Louisiana Superlative modern art museum with a huge children's wing and plenty of outdoor running space. (p123)

Statens Museum for Kunst Denmark's National Gallery offers a sketching room, weekend workshops for kids, plus a monthly kids' day. (p88)

Outdoor Thrills

Tivoli Gardens The world's most charming amusement park, with laser shows, fireworks and rides from the tame to the insane. (p24)

GoBoat Kids can play 'trash pirates' on solar-powered boats, collecting rubbish for a reward. (p78)

Islands Brygge Havnebadet Wade, bomb or swim with a summertime dip at Copenhagen's favourite harbour pool. (p139)

Kongens Have Catch a summertime puppet show in Christian IV's old backyard. (p87)

For Historical Insight

Nationalmuseet Sail a ship or be a knight in the National Museum's interactive Children's Museum. (p28)

Rosenborg Slot Stomp through a gingerbread-style castle, complete with guards, moat and basement crowns. (p84)

Mystery Makers Active, family-friendly mystery games that see teams searching for clues in historic locations. (p68)

Rundetårn Climb Christian IV's curious round tower for a game of 'spot the landmarks'. (p48)

☑ Top Tips

▶ Larger bicycle-rental outfits have kids' trailers and kids' bikes for rent.

▶ Kids aged 12 to 15 years pay half-price on public transport. An adult with a valid ticket can take two children under the age of 12 for free.

▶ See www.visit copenhagen.com for family-friendly activities.

Best
Architecture

Copenhagen's architectural cache is rich and diverse, spanning many centuries and architectural styles. Despite its age, this is a city not short of contemporary edge, its Renaissance, baroque and National Romantic treasures sharing the spotlight with modernist icons and innovative just-built marvels that inspire urban planners across the globe.

ANGEL VILLALBA/GETTY IMAGES ©

Historical Overview

Copenhagen's architectural legacy begins with Bishop Absalon's 12th-century fortress, its ruins visible beneath Christiansborg Slot. 'Builder King' Christian IV embarked on an extraordinary building program in the 17th century that includes Børsen, Rundetårn and Rosenborg Slot. Rococo delights include Amalienborg Slot and Marmorkirken, while Rådhus (City Hall) is a standout example of the National Romantic style – inspired by Scandinavian heritage and popular at the turn of last century.

Rosenborg Slot A petite castle built in the Dutch Renaissance style. (p84)

Christiansborg Slot Copenhagen's boldest neobaroque statement. (p36)

Rundetårn Christian IV's astronomical tower, complete with equestrian staircase. (p48)

Børsen A Dutch Renaissance stock exchange with rooftop dragons. (p42)

Det Kongelige Bibliotek The 'Black Diamond' heralded a new era for Copenhagen's waterfront. (p41)

Operaen Copenhagen's harbourfront opera house divides opinion. (p81)

☑ Top Tip

▶ Newly relocated to architect Rem Koolhaas' Blox building, the **Dansk Arkitektur Center** (www.dac.dk; Frederiksholms Kanal 30; exhibition adult/child 40kr/free, 5-9pm Wed free; ⏲exhibition & bookshop 10am-5pm Mon, Tue & Thu-Sun, to 9pm Wed; 🚌66, 🚢Det Kongelige Bibliotek) houses a notable book and design store, hosts exhibitions on architecture, and also runs architecture-themed walking tours of the city in the summer. See the website for details.

Best
Design

Is there a more design-conscious nation than Denmark, or a more design-obsessed capital than Copenhagen? Sure, the Italians like a nice sofa and the French have their frocks, but in Denmark design excellence runs deeper than that. From its restaurant and hotel interiors to its cycling overpasses, one of Copenhagen's most inspirational qualities is its love and mastery of the applied arts.

Kaare Klint: Danish Design Pioneer

While modern Danish design bloomed in the 1950s, its roots are firmly planted in the 1920s and the work of pioneering Danish modernist Kaare Klint (1888–1954). The architect spent much of his career studying the human form and modified a number of chair designs for added functionality. Klint's obsession with functionality, accessibility and attention to detail would ultimately drive and define Denmark's mid-20th-century design scene and its broader design legacy.

Designmuseum Danmark Delve into the history and iconic pieces of Denmark's design heritage. (p60)

Klassik Moderne Møbelkunst A retail repository for the country's most celebrated chairs, tables and more. (p69)

Hay House Furniture, homewares and gifts from new-school Nordic talent. (p55)

Designer Zoo Not just a design store but a work space for talented local designers and artisans. (p119)

Illums Bolighus All the biggest names in design on four inspiring levels. (p55)

Höst The urban-rustic interior of this New Nordic nosh spot has swagged international awards. (p94)

JARL AXEL/DESIGNMUSEUM DANMARK ©

☑ **Top Tip**

▶ Held in late May or early June, the **3 Days of Design** (http://3daysofdesign. dk; ⏲May/Jun) festival sees dozens of venues, from furniture and design stores to cafes and Designmuseum Danmark, host special design-themed events open to the public. These include talks, tours and product launches.

Normann Copenhagen This converted cinema is now a showcase for modern industrial design. (p107)

Best
Festivals & Events

Bass-thumping block parties and saxy jazz, pot-stirring celebrity chefs, groundbreaking films and documentaries, and a rainbow-coloured Pride parade: Copenhagen's social calendar is a buzz-inducing, toe-tapping affair. Sunshine, sleet or snow, you're bound to find a reason to head out and celebrate the finer things in life.

BIOSTRUP/GETTY IMAGES ©

Best for Culture Vultures

Kulturnatten (Culture Night; www.kulturnatten.dk; ⏱Oct) Late-night art and culture, usually on the second Friday in October.

Kulturhavn (www.kulturhavn.dk; ⏱Aug) Three days of mostly free harbourside events in early August.

Code Art Fair (www.codeartfair.dk; ⏱Aug/Sep) A four-day international art fair held in late August and/or early September.

Best for Music

Copenhagen Jazz Festival (www.jazz.dk; ⏱Jul) Ten massive days of world-class jazz in early July. A winter edition is held in February.

Copenhagen Blues Festival (www.copenhagenbluesfestival.dk; ⏱Sep/Oct) Five days of international blues in late September or early October.

Strøm (www.stromcph.dk; ⏱Aug) A five-day electronic music festival in August.

Distortion (www.cphdistortion.dk; ⏱May/Jun) Five heady days of club and block parties in late May and early June.

Best for Gluttons

Copenhagen Cooking & Food Festival (www.copenhagencooking.dk; ⏱Aug) Scandinavia's largest food festival runs in August.

Ølfestival (http://beerfestival.dk; ⏱May) A three-day beer fest in May,

☑ **Top Tip**

▶ The best sources of up-to-date info on events are www.visitcopenhagen.com and www.aok.dk (in Danish). Also useful is the English-language Copenhagen Post (www.cphpost.dk).

showcasing Danish and international producers.

Best for Film Buffs

CPH:PIX (www.cphpix.dk; ⏱Sep/Oct) Copenhagen's feature film festival runs for two weeks in September or October.

CPH:DOX (www.cphdox.dk; ⏱Mar) An acclaimed, 11-day documentary film festival in March.

Survival Guide

Before You Go   **146**

When to Go 146

Book Your Stay 146

Arriving in Copenhagen   **147**

Copenhagen Airport 147

Central Station 148

Søndre Frihavn 148

Getting Around   **148**

Bus.............................. 148

Metro............................ 148

Bicycle 148

Train 149

Boat............................. 149

Essential Information   **149**

Business Hours 149

Discount Cards................... 150

Electricity 150

Money 150

Public Holidays 150

Safe Travel 151

Telephone 151

Toilets 151

Tourist Information 151

Travellers with Disabilities........ 151

Visas 151

Survival Guide

Before You Go

When to Go

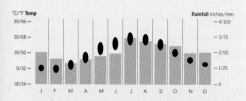

°C/°F Temp
- 30/86
- 20/68
- 10/50
- 0/32
- -10/14

Rainfall inches/mm
- 4/100
- 3/75
- 2/50
- 1/25
- 0

J F M A M J J A S O N D

➡ **Winter (Dec–Feb)**
Short days and frigid temperatures. Christmas lights, markets and *gløgg* (mulled wine) keep spirits up in December.

➡ **Spring (Mar–May)**
Milder weather usually arrives around April. Outdoor attractions begin to reopen.

➡ **Summer (Jun–Aug)**
The best time to visit, with long daylight hours and plenty of outdoor festivals and events.

➡ **Autumn (Sep–Nov)**
Crisp days and brilliant bursts of red and gold illuminate the city's parks. November heralds the winter gloom.

Book Your Stay

☑ **Top Tip** The rates of some hostels and most midrange and top-end hotels are based on supply and demand, with daily fluctuations. In most cases, booking early guarantees the best deal.

➡ It's a good idea to book in advance – rooms in many of the most popular midrange hotels fill quickly.

➡ Copenhagen's hostels often fill early in summer so it's best to make reservations in advance.

➡ You will need a hostelling card to get the advertised rates at hostels belonging to the Danhostel organisation.

➡ The Copenhagen Visitors Centre can make same-day hotel reservations for a fee (100kr).

Useful Websites

Lonely Planet (www.lonelyplanet.com/denmark/copenhagen/hotels) Author-reviewed accommodation options.

Hay4You (www.hay4you.com) Offers self-catering apartments across the city, including in the historic centre, Christianshavn and Vesterbro.

Copenhagen Visitors Centre (www.visitcopenhagen.com) Can book last-minute accommodation for visitors for a 100kr booking fee.

Best Budget

Generator Hostel (www.generatorhostel.com) Contemporary dorms, private rooms and a central location.

Copenhagen Downtown Hostel (www.copenhagendowntown.com) Gigs, city walks and free dinners in the historic centre.

Urban House (https://urbanhouse.me) A Vesterbro hostel close to hip eateries and with its own tattoo parlour.

Best Midrange

Hotel Alexandra (http://hotelalexandra.dk) A chic yet homey hotel with cult-status furniture.

Babette Guldsmeden (https://guldsmedenhotels.com) Crisp rooms and organic breakfasts near the Royal Palace.

Hotel Danmark (www.brochner-hotels.com) Snug, stylish rooms, free evening vino and a rooftop terrace.

CPH Living (https://www.cphliving.com) A light-filled floating hotel right on Copenhagen harbour.

Best Top End

Hotel d'Angleterre (www.dangleterre.com) History-steeped luxury and a celebrity fan base near Nyhavn.

Hotel Nimb (www.nimb.dk) Unique luxury suites with views of a 19th-century pleasure garden.

Radisson BLU Royal Hotel (www.radissonblue.com) A mid-century icon created by design deity Arne Jacobsen.

Arriving in Copenhagen

Copenhagen Airport

Metro The 24-hour metro (www.m.dk) runs every four to 20 minutes between the airport arrival terminal (the station is called Lufthavnen) and the eastern side of the city centre. It does not stop at København H (Central Station) but is handy for Christianshavn, the city centre and Nyhavn (get off at Kongens Nytorv for Nyhavn). Journey time to Kongens Nytorv is 14 minutes (36kr).

Train Trains (www.dsb.dk) connect the airport arrival terminal to Copenhagen Central Station (Københavns Hovedbanegården, commonly known as København H) around every 10 to 20 minutes. Journey time is 14 minutes (36kr).

Taxi Journey time from the airport to the city centre is about 20 minutes, depending on traffic. Expect to pay 250kr to 300kr.

Central Station

All regional and international trains arrive at and depart from Central Station, located opposite Tivoli Gardens in the heart of the city. Trains run to the airport every 10 to 20 minutes, with less frequent services overnight.

Søndre Frihavn

Søndre Frihavn port is situated 2km north of central Copenhagen and serves ferries to and from Oslo, Norway. From Central Station, catch the S-train to Nordhavn station, from where the port is a 10- to 15-minute walk. Bus 26 connects the port to many parts of the city.

Getting Around

Bus

➡ City buses are frequent, convenient and run by Movia (https://www.moviatrafik.dk/). Single tickets can be purchased on board. If using a Rejsekort, tap on when boarding the bus and tap off when exiting.

➡ Primary bus routes have an 'A' after their route number (eg: 1A, 2A) and run around the clock, every three to seven minutes in peak times (7am to 9pm and 3.30pm to 5.30pm) and around every 10 minutes at other times.

➡ S-buses (buses with an 'S' after their route number) run every five to 10 minutes in peak times and around every 20 minutes at other times. S-buses have fewer stops than A-buses and usually run between 6pm and 1am.

➡ Night buses (marked with an 'N' after their route number) run between 1am and 5am.

➡ The free Copenhagen city maps at the tourist office show bus routes (with numbers) and are very useful.

Metro

➡ Currently consists of two lines (M1 and M2). A city circle (Cityringen) line is due for completion in 2019.

➡ Metro trains run around the clock, with a frequency of two to four minutes in peak times, three to six minutes during the day and on weekends, and seven to 20 minutes at night.

➡ Both lines connect Nørreport with Kongens Nytorv and Christianshavn. Line M2 (yellow line) runs to the airport.

➡ The rechargeable Rejsekort travel card is valid on the metro.

➡ See www.m.dk for more information.

Bicycle

➡ The city-wide rental system **Bycyklen** (www.bycyklen.dk; per 1hr 30kr) offers high-tech 'Smart Bikes' with GPS, multi-speed electric motors and locks. The bikes must by paid for by credit card via the website or the bike's touchscreen.

➡ Bikes can be carried free on S-trains, but are banned at Nørreport station on weekdays between 7am and 8.30am and between 3.30pm and 5pm. Enter train carriages with the large white bicycle graphic on the windows. Keep your bike behind the line in the designated bicycle area. Stay with the bike at all times.

➡ Bikes can be carried on the metro (except from 7am to 9am and from 3.30pm to 5.30pm on weekdays). Bike tickets (13kr) are required on metro and city bus

Tickets & Passes

Copenhagen's bus, metro, S-train and Harbour Bus network has an integrated ticket system based on seven geographical zones. Most of your travel within the city will be within two zones. Travel between the city and airport covers three zones.

The cheapest ticket (billet) covers two zones, offers unlimited transfers and is valid for one hour (adult/12 to 15 years 24/12kr). An adult with a valid ticket can take two children under the age of 12 free of charge.

Alternatively, you can purchase a **Rejsekort** (www.rejsekort.dk), a touch-on, touch-off smart card valid for all zones. Available from the Rejsekort machines at metro stations, Central Station or the airport, the card costs 180kr (80kr for the card and 100kr in credit).

The tourist-saver **Copenhagen Card** (www.copenhagencard.com; adult/child 10-15yr 24hr 389/199kr, 48hr 549/279kr, 72hr 659/329kr, 120hr 889/449kr) includes unlimited public transport throughout the greater region of Copenhagen (including the airport).

services. Purchase bike tickets at metro and S-train stations; they are not sold on buses.

Train

➡ Known locally as S-tog, Copenhagen's suburban train network runs seven lines through Central Station (København H). The S-train runs between Copenhagen Airport and Central Station.

➡ Services run every four to 20 minutes from approximately 5am to 12.30am. All-night services run hourly on Friday and Saturday (half-hourly on line F).

➡ The rechargeable Rejsekort travel card is valid on S-train services.

Boat

➡ Movia operates the city's yellow commuter ferries, known as Harbour Buses.

➡ Route 991 runs north along the harbour, 992 runs south. There are 10 harbour stops, including Det Kongelige Bibliotek (Royal Library), Nyhavn and Operaen (Opera House).

➡ Route 993 serves as a shuttle service between Nyhavn, Experimentarium and Operaen from 9am to 6pm on weekdays. From 6pm to 11pm, it only runs between Nyhavn and Operaen.

➡ The rechargeable Rejsekort travel card is valid on Harbour Buses.

Essential Information

Business Hours

Opening hours vary throughout the year. We've provided high-season opening hours; hours generally decrease in the shoulder and low seasons.

Banks 10am–4pm Monday to Friday (to 5.30pm or 6pm Thursday)

Bars 4pm–midnight, to 2am or later Friday and Saturday (clubs on weekends may open until 5am)

Boutiques 10am or 11am–6pm Monday to Friday, to 4pm Saturday, some open Sunday

Cafes 8am–5pm or 6pm

Department stores 10am–8pm

Restaurants noon–10pm or 11pm

Supermarkets 8am–9pm or 10pm (some open 7am; a few open 24 hours)

Discount Cards

The **Copenhagen Card** (www.copenhagencard.com; adult/child 10-15yr 24hr 389/199kr, 48hr 549/279kr, 72hr 659/329kr, 120hr 889/449kr) gives you access to 79 museums and attractions, as well as free public transport. Each adult card includes up to two children aged under 10. The card can be purchased at the Copenhagen Visitors Centre, as well as at the airport information desk, the tourist information centre inside Central Station, and at various

hotels and 7-Eleven stores. You can also purchase the card online.

Electricity

230V/50Hz

Money

Credit Cards

➜ Credit cards such as Visa and MasterCard are

widely accepted in Denmark; American Express and Diners Club less so.

➜ In many places (hotels, petrol stations, restaurants, shops) a surcharge may be imposed on foreign cards (up to 3.75%). If there is a surcharge, it must be advertised (eg on the menu, at reception).

Public Holidays

New Year's Day (Nytårsdag) 1 January

Maundy Thursday (Skærtorsdag) Thursday before Easter

Good Friday (Langfredag) Friday before Easter

Easter Day (Påskedag) Sunday in March or April

Easter Monday (2. påskedag) Day after Easter

Great Prayer Day (Stor Bededag) Fourth Friday after Easter

Ascension Day (Kristi Himmelfartsdag) Sixth Thursday after Easter

Whitsunday (Pinsedag) Seventh Sunday after Easter

Whitmonday (2. pinsedag) Seventh Monday after Easter

Money-saving Tips

➜ Some museums offer free entry, either daily or once weekly.

➜ Seniors and students qualify for discounts on some transport fares and museum entry fees, but you'll need to show proof of student status or age.

➜ Self-catering at supermarkets and markets can help keep food costs down.

➜ Consider getting around on foot – compact Copenhagen was made for walking.

Constitution Day
(Grundlovsdag) 5 June

Christmas Eve (Juleaften) 24 December (from noon)

Christmas Day (Juledag) 25 December

Boxing Day (2. juledag) 26 December

Safe Travel

Copenhagen is a very safe city, but you should always employ common sense.

➡ Keep your belongings in sight, particularly in busy places.

➡ Keep clear of the busy bike lanes that run beside roads; they are easy to wander onto (and straight into the path of cyclists).

Telephone

☑ **Top Tip** If you're coming from outside Europe, check that your phone will work in Europe's GSM 900/1800 network (US phones work on a different frequency).

Useful Numbers

Local Directory Assistance (☏118)

International Directory Assistance (☏113)

Toilets

➡ Public toilets are generally easy to find and most are free to use.

➡ Handy places to find them include department stores, libraries and major train stations.

➡ Museums, cafes and restaurants have toilets for their guests.

Tourist Information

Copenhagen Visitors Centre (☏70 22 24 42; www.visitcopenhagen.com; Vesterbrogade 4A, Vesterbro; ⏰9am-8pm Mon-Fri, to 6pm Sat & Sun Jul & Aug, reduced hours rest of year; ☏; ☐2A, 6A, 12, 14, 26, 250S, Ⓢ København H) Copenhagen's excellent and informative information centre has a cafe and lounge with free wi-fi; it also sells the **Copenhagen Card** (www.copenhagencard.com; adult/child 10-15yr 24hr 389/199kr, 48hr 549/279kr, 72hr 659/329kr, 120hr 889/449kr).

Travellers with Disabilities

➡ Copenhagen, and Denmark in general, are improving accessibility all the time, although accessibility is still not ubiquitous. The official www.visitcopenhagen.com website lists accessible sights, hotels and restaurants, as well as practical tips and useful links. To access the page, click on 'Plan Your Stay', then 'Travel Trade' followed by 'Accessible Copenhagen'.

➡ A useful resource is God Adgang (Good Access; www.godadgang.dk), which lists service providers who have had their facilities registered and labelled for accessibility.

Visas

➡ No entry visa is needed by citizens of EU and Nordic countries.

➡ Citizens of the USA, Canada, Australia and New Zealand need a valid passport to enter Denmark, but they don't need a visa for tourist stays of less than 90 days.

➡ Citizens of many African, South American, Asian and former Soviet bloc countries do require a visa. See www.newtodenmark.dk.

Language

Most of the sounds in Danish have equivalents in English, and by reading our pronunciation guides as if they were English, you're sure to be understood. There are short and long versions of each vowel, and additional 'combined vowels' or diphthongs. Consonants can be 'swallowed' and even omitted completely, creating (together with vowels) a glottal stop or *stød steudh* which sounds rather like the Cockney pronunciation of the 'tt' in 'bottle'. Note that *ai* is pronounced as in 'aisle', *aw* as in 'saw', *eu* as the 'u' in 'nurse', *ew* as the 'ee' in 'see' with rounded lips, *ow* as in 'how', *dh* as the 'th' in 'that', and *r* is trilled. The stressed syllables are in italics in our pronunciation guides.

To enhance your trip with a phrase-book, visit **lonelyplanet.com**.

Basics

Hello.
Goddag.　　　　　　go·da

Goodbye.
Farvel.　　　　　　faar·vel

Yes./No.
Ja./Nej.　　　　　　ya/nai

Please.
Vær så venlig.　　　ver saw ven·lee

Thank you.
Tak.　　　　　　　taak

You're welcome.
Selv tak.　　　　　sel taak

Excuse me.
Undskyld mig.　　　awn·skewl mai

Sorry.
Undskyld.　　　　　awn·skewl

How are you?
Hvordan går det?　　vor·dan gawr dey

Good, thanks.
Godt, tak.　　　　　got taak

What's your name?
Hvad hedder　　　　va hey·dha
du?　　　　　　　doo

My name is ...
Mit navn er ...　　　mit nown ir ...

Do you speak English?
Taler du　　　　　ta·la dee/doo
engelsk?　　　　　eng·elsk

I don't understand.
Jeg forstår ikke.　　yai for·stawr i·ke

Eating & Drinking

What would you recommend?
Hvad du　　　　　va doo
anbefale?　　　　　an·bey·fa·le

Do you have vegetarian food?
Har I　　　　　　haar ee
vegetarmad?　　　　vey·ge·taar·madh

Cheers!
Skål!　　　　　　skawl

I'd like (the) ..., please.
Jeg vil gerne　　　yai vil gir·ne
have ..., tak.　　　ha ... taak

bill
regningen　　　　rai·ning·en

drink list
vinkortet　　　　veen·kor·tet

menu
menuen　　　　　me·new·en

Emergencies

Help!
Hjælp!   yelp

Go away!
Gå væk!   gaw vek

Call ...!
Ring efter ...!   ring ef·ta ...

  a doctor
  en læge   in le·ye

  the police
  politiet   poh·lee·tee·et

It's an emergency!
Det er et   dey ir it
nødstilfælde!   neudhs·til·fe·le

I'm lost.
Jeg er faret vild.   yai ir faa·ret veel

I'm sick.
Jeg er syg.   yai ir sew

It hurts here.
Det gør ondt her.   dey geur awnt heyr

I'm allergic to...
Jeg er allergisk   yai ir a·ler·geesk
over for...   o·va for...

Where's the toilet?
Hvor er toilettet?   vor ir toy·le·tet

Shopping & Services

I'm looking for ...
Jeg leder efter ...   yai li·dha ef·ta ...

How much is it?
Hvor meget   vor maa·yet
koster det?   kos·ta dey

Can I have a look?
Må jeg se?   maw yai sey

Time & Numbers

What time is it?
Hvad er klokken?   va ir klo·ken

1	*en*	in
2	*to*	toh
3	*tre*	trey
4	*fire*	feer
5	*fem*	fem
6	*seks*	seks
7	*syv*	sew
8	*otte*	aw·te
9	*ni*	nee
10	*ti*	tee
100	*hundrede*	hoon·re·dhe
1000	*tusind*	too·sen

Transport & Directions

Where's the ...?
Hvor er ...?   vor ir ...

What's the address?
Hvad er adressen?   va ir a·draa·sen

How do I get there?
Hvordan kommer   vor·dan ko·ma
jeg derhen?   yai deyr·hen

Please take me to (this address).
Vær venlig at   ver ven·lee at
køre mig   keu·re mai
til (denne adresse).   til (de·ne a·draa·se)

Please stop here.
Venligst stop her.   ven·leest stop heyr

boat	*båden*	baw·dhen
bicycle	*cykel*	see·kel
bus	*bussen*	boo·sen
plane	*flyet*	flew·et
train	*toget*	taw·et

Behind the Scenes

Send Us Your Feedback

We love to hear from travellers – your comments help make our books better. We read every word, and we guarantee that your feedback goes straight to the authors. Visit **lonelyplanet.com/contact** to submit your updates and suggestions.

    Note: We may edit, reproduce and incorporate your comments in Lonely Planet products such as guidebooks, websites and digital products, so let us know if you don't want your comments reproduced or your name acknowledged. For a copy of our privacy policy visit lonelyplanet.com/privacy.

Our Readers

Thanks to the travellers who used the last edition and wrote to us with helpful hints, useful advice and interesting anecdotes:
Belén Arranz, David Grumett, Ryan Lawson, Susan Rieder, Jake Sullivan, Gillian Weale

Christian Struckmann Irgens, Mads Lind, Mia Hjorth Lunde and Jens Lunde, Mary-ann Gardner and Lambros Hajisava, Sophie Lind and Kasper Monrad, Anne Marie Nielsen, Sanna Klein Hedegaard Hansen and Carolyn Bain. In-house, many thanks to Gemma Graham.

Cristian's Thanks

For their priceless insight, generosity and friendship, *tusind tak* to Martin Kalhøj, Mette Cecilie Smedegaard,

Acknowledgements

Cover photograph: Rosenborg Slot, Maurizio Rellini/4Corners ©

This Book

This 4th edition of Lonely Planet's *Pocket Copenhagen* was written by Cristian Bonetto, as was the previous edition. This guidebook was produced by the following:

Destination Editor
Gemma Graham

Product Editor Shona Gray

Cartographer Valentina Kremenchutskaya

Book Designer
Lauren Egan

Cover Researcher
Naomi Parker

Assisting Editors Imogen Bannister, Michelle Bennett, Hannah Cartmel, Katie Connolly, Jodie Martire, Kristin Odijk, Genna Patterson, Maja Vatrić

Thanks to Claire Naylor, Kirsten Rawlings, Jessica Ryan, Tony Wheeler

Index

See also separate subindexes for:

- Eating p157
- Drinking p157
- Entertainment p158
- Shopping p158

A

accommodation 146
activities
  baths 107
  boating 78
  cycling 50, 119, 148-9
Amalienborg Slot 64
amusement parks, see
  Tivoli Gardens
Aquila 25
architecture 105, 142
**Assistens
  Kirkegård 99**

B

BaNanna Park 128
Basco5 Mural 128
bicycling, see cycling
boat travel 149
Børsen 42
Botanisk Have 93
Brumleby 107
budgeting 16
bus travel 148
business hours 149

C

Carlsberg Brewery 121
cell phones 16
children, travel with 141

Sights 000
Map Pages **000**

Christiania 72-5, 74
Christians Kirke 78
**Christiansborg
  Ridebane 126**
**Christiansborg Slot
  Tower 38**
**Christiansborg Slot
  36-9**
**Christiansborg
  Slotskirke 38**
Christianshavn
  70-81, **76**
  drinking 80-1
  entertainment 81
  food 78, 80
  highlights 71
  itineraries 71
  sights 72-8
  transport 71
Cisternerne 121
climate 146
Copenhagen
  map **18-19**
**Copenhagen
  Zoo 121**
costs 16, 150
credit cards 150
currency 16
cycling 50, 148-9

D

**Dansk Arkitektur
  Center 33**
**Dansk Jødisk
  Museum 42**
Davids Samling 93

De Kongelige
  Repræsentation-
  slokaler 36-7
**De Kongelige
  Stalde 42**
Den Grå Hal 75
design 54, 143
**Designmuseum
  Denmark 60-1**
**Det Kongelige
  Bibliotek 41**
**Det Kongelige
  Biblioteks Have
  126**
disabilities, travellers
  with 151
discount cards 150
drinking & nightlife 136,
  see also individual
  neighbourhoods,
  Drinking & Nightlife
  subindex
**Dronning Louises
  Bro 105**
Dyssen 73

E

eco-friendly 101
electricity 150
entertainment 137,
  see also individual
  neighbourhoods,
  Entertainment
  subindex

F

festivals & events 144
fireworks 26

food 79, 90-1, 134-5,
  see also individual
  neighbourhoods,
  Eating subindex
Frederiksberg Have
  120-1, **120**
  transport 120
free activities 139

H

Hans Christian
  Andersen 66
highlights 8-11, 12-13
Hirschsprung 94
history 29, 39
hygge 26, 32, 33, 51, 52,
  67, 80
  Copenhagen's best
  138

I

**Islands Brygge
  Havnebadet 139**
itineraries 14-15, 126-9,
  see also individual
  neighbourhoods

J

**Jægersborggade
  129**
**Jens Olsen's World
  Clock 31**

K

Kastellet 65
**Kunstforeningen GL
  Strand 48**

Kunsthal Charlottenberg 65

L

language 16, 152-3
Latin Quarter 48
Little Mermaid 66
live music
  Jazzhouse 53
  Jazzhouse Montmarte 53
  Mojo 33
local life 12-13
  Frederiksberg 120-1
  Torvellaherne KBH 90-1
  Østerbro 106-7,
  Værnedamsvej 110-11
Louisiana Museum of Modern Art 122-3

M

Marble Bridge 126
markets
  Frederiksberg Loppetorv 121
  Nørrebro Loppemarked 105
  Torvehallerne KBH 90-1
  Westmarket 115
Marmorkirken 64
mobile phones 16
money 16, 150
museums & galleries 130-1, see individual museums & galleries
music 33, 42, 53

N

Nationalmuseet 28-9

new Nordic
  cuisine 79
  108 78
  AOC 66
  Bror 32
  Höst 94
  Kadeau 78
  Marv & Ben 50
  Nørrebro Bryghus 104
  Pony 117
  Relæ 101
  Søren K 43
Nikolaj Kunsthal 49
Nørrebro 96-105, **98**
  drinking 102-4
  food 99-100
  highlights 97
  itineraries 97
  shopping 104-5
  sights 99
  transport 97
Nørreport 82-95, **92**
  drinking 95
  food 90-1, 94
  highlights 83
  itineraries 83
  sights 84-90, 93-4
  shopping 95
  transport 83
Ny Carlsberg Glyptotek 31
Nyhavn 58-69, **62-3**
  drinking 68
  entertainment 68-9
  food 66-7
  highlights 59
  itineraries 59
  shopping 69
  sights 60-5
  transport 59

O

Odinsgade Murals 129
Olufsvej 107
Østerbro 106-7, **106**
  sights 107
  transport 106
Overgaden 77

P

pantomime 26
phrasebook, see language
public holidays 150

R

Rådhus 31-2
Rosenborg Slot 84-7
Rosenvænget 107
Royal Quarter 58-69, **62-3**
  drinking 68
  entertainment 68-9
  food 66-7
  highlights 59
  itineraries 59
  shopping 69
  sights 60-5
  transport 59
Ruinerne under Christiansborg 37
Rundetårn 48
Rutschebanen 25

S

safety 151
Shooting Range Wall 114
shopping 132-3, see also individual neighbourhoods, Shopping subindex
Slotsholmen 34-43, **40**
  food 43

highlights 35
itineraries 35
sights 36-43
transport 35
Sortedams Sø 107
Stadens Museum for Kunst 73
Star Flyer 25
Staten Museum for Kunst 88-9
Strædet 49
street art 114
Strøget 44-57, **46-7**
  drinking 51-3
  entertainment 53
  food 50-1
  highlights 45
  itineraries 45
  shopping 55-7
  sights 48-9
  transport 45
  subway 148
Superkilen 128

T

Teatermuseet 38
telephone services 16
theatre 26, 69
Thorvaldsens Museum 41
tickets 149
time 16
Tivoli 22-33, **30**
  drinking 33
  entertainment 33
  food 32
  highlights 23
  itineraries 23
  sights 28-32
  transport 23
Tivoli Gardens 24-7, 2?
toilets 151
Tøjhusmuseet 43

Sights 000
Map Pages **000**

top sights 8-11
Torvehallerne KBH 90-1, 91
tourist information 151
tours 33, 140
train travel 149
transport 17, 147-8

V

V1 Gallery 114
Værnedamsvej 110-11
Vesterbro 108-19, **112-13**
  drinking 117-8
  entertainment 119
  food 114-7
  highlights 109
  itineraries 109
  local life 109
  shopping 119
  sights 114
  transport 109
viewpoints
  Christiansborg Slot Tower 38
  Kastellet 65
  Mamorkirken 64
  Ny Carlsberg Glyptotek 32
  Rådhus 48
  Rundetårn 48
  Vor Frelsers Kirke 77
Vilhelm Dahlerup 105
visas 151
Vor Frelsers Kirke 77
Vor Frue Kirke 48

W

walks 126-9
weather 146
websites 16, 146-7

Eating

108 78

A

Aamanns Takeaway 89
AOC 66
Atelier September 94

B

Barr 80
Bæst 100
Big Apple 85
Bror 32

C

Café Halvvejen 51
Cafe Wilder 80

D

District Tonkin 66
DØP 51

F

Fischer 107

G

Gemyse 25
Gorm's 67
Granola 110
Grød 90
Grøften 25

H

Hallernes Smørrebrød 91
Hija de Sanchez 116
Höst 94

K

Kadeau 78
Kanal Cafée 32
Klint Cafe 61
Kødbyens Fiskebar 115

L

La Glace 51

M

Manfreds og Vin 102
Marv & Ben 50
Meyers Bageri 67
Mirabelle 100
Møller 102
Morgenstedet 80

N

Nose2Tail 116

O

Øieblikket 43
Øl & Brød 116
Omegn 90
Orangeriet 85
Oysters & Grill 99

P

Paté Paté 114
Pixie 107
Pluto 61, 94
Pony 117

R

Rebel 66
Relæ 100
Restaurant Mes 32

S

Schønnemann 50
Siciliansk Is 117
Sokkelund 121
Søren K 43

T

Tårnet 43
The Market 50

Tommi's Burger Joint 117

U

Unika 90
Union Kitchen 67

W

WarPigs 117
WestMarket 115

Drinking & Nightlife

1105 52

B

Bankeråt 95
Bastard Café 52
Bibendum 95
Brus 102

C

Christianshavns Bådudlejning og Caf 80
Coffee Collective (Frederiksburg) 103
Coffee Collective (Nørreport) 90
Coffee Collective (Nørrebro) 103
Culture Box 95

D

Democratic Coffee 52
Den Plettede Gris 81
Den Vandrette 68
Dyrehaven 118

F

Fermentoren 118
Forloren Espresso 67

K

Kassen 104
Kind of Blue 104

L

Lidkoeb 117
Living Room 33

M

Mesteren & Lærlingen 118
Mikkeller & Friends 102
Mikkeller Bar 117
Mother Wine 52

N

Nebbiolo 68
Nimb Bar 33
Noorbohandelen 91
Nørrebro Bryghus 104

P

P2 by Malbeck 104

R

Ruby 52
Rust 103

S

Sort Kaffe & Vinyl 118

V

Ved Stranden 10 51

☆ Entertainment

Cinemateket 55
Det Kongelige Teater 68
Jazzhouse 53
Jazzhus Montmartre 53

Loppen 75
Mojo 33
Mystery Makers 68
Operaen 81
Skuespilhuset 69
Tivoli Koncertsa 33
Vega Live 119

🛍 Shopping

Baum und Pferdgarten 56
Designer Zoo 119
Dora 111
Frederiksberg Loppetorv 121
Gågron! 105
Han Kjøbenhavn 57
Hay House 55
Illums Bolighus 55

Juuls Vin og Spiritus 111
Klassik Moderne Møbelkunst 69
Kyoto 119
NN07 56
Normann Copenhagen 107
Nørrebro Loppemarked 105
Playtype 111
Posterland 56
Prag 111
Samsøe & Samsøe 111
Stilleben 55
Stine Goya 95
Storm 56
Vanishing Point 104
Wood Wood 57

Sights 000
Map Pages **000**